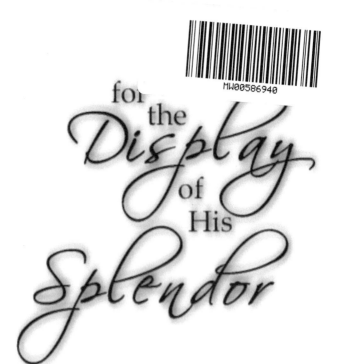

for
the
Display
of
His
Splendor

for the Display of His Splendor

Dear Betty~

Live for His Splendor!

Norma Steven

Norma Steven

Unless otherwise noted, Scripture quotations are
taken from the New International Version of the
Bible, Copyright © 1973, 1978, 1984, by International
Bible Society.

Printed in the United States of America

ISBN: 0-9769634-3-4
Library of Congress Cataloging in-Publication Data is available
Steven, Norma
For the Display of His Splendor / by Norma Steven
ISBN: 0-9769634-3-4
Biography, Autobiography, Missionary, Memoirs

Interior design by Rick Lindholtz

On the Tracks Media, LLC
onthetracksmedia.com

Dedication

For my children and their spouses:
Wendy & Greg Asimakoupoulos
Dave Steven
Lee & Paula Steven
Karen & Chris Romig;
my grandchildren and their spouses
and my great grandchildren.
May they all, and those to come,
desire to live for the
display of God's splendor
until we are reunited in glory
with our blessed Savior

They are the shoots I have planted,
the work of my hands,
for the display of my splendor.
Isaiah 60:21b

They will be called oaks of righteousness,
a planting of the Lord
for the display of His splendor.
Isaiah 61:3b

Acknowledgements

As with all writing adventures, it is not done alone. I am, therefore, most grateful to our daughter Wendy and her husband Greg Asimakoupoulos for their financial partnership in publishing this memoir. And I am particularly grateful to Wendy for her patience, encouragement and careful editing and suggestions. To my husband Hugh who from the beginning encouraged me to tell my story. Lastly, I am grateful to God for giving me these bonus years as a testimony and legacy for our family and friends to acknowledge God's faithfulness for over ninety years as we have endeavored to live for The Display of His Splendor.

Norma Steven
Santa Ana, California,
2021

Contents

1

I Remember

P.D. James, the great mystery novelist, wrote in her partial autobiography, *A Time to be Earnest*,[1] "Any writing, if it is worth doing, requires care." Perhaps it is this "care" that has kept me from writing a history for my family. To write a good history or memoir is not just relating a series of facts and incidents. It takes time, effort and care to add feeling, emotion and drama, and I didn't feel I had the time or ability to do this. However, I hope what follows, is a readable, enjoyable account of my early life, my 70 years with husband Hugh Steven, our family, and also some early history of my parents, Hilda (nee Otto) and Harry Van Boeyen.

In thinking about where to begin, I'm depending on what my mother wrote in my baby book. I was born in Grace Hospital in Vancouver, B.C., Canada on July 8, 1931 and named Norma Isobel Van Boeyen. My weight was 7 lbs. 5 oz., but there is no record anywhere of my length. I remember my mother telling me it was a very hot day and the nurses had trouble locating her doctor. She had to hold me in until he arrived, and it was "difficult!"

From the beginning, my hair was brown. My eyes changed from blue to brown. I smiled at one week old. I

---

[1] P.D. James, *A Time to be Earnest*, Alfred and Knopf, New York, 2000. p.1.

have a sneaking suspicion it may have just been gas! I began to crawl at ten months, I got my first tooth at 13 months, at 15 months my first kiss was given to my sister Mabel, and that's when I took my first step alone.

I'm sure I've given you more statistics than you wanted to know but I need to tell you my first sentence at 18 months was "Jesus loves me." As son Lee used to call me, I was "Holy Boly" right from the start! In fact, my mother said I would keep them awake at night singing *Jesus Loves Me* and top that off with the first line of *Trust and Obey*.

At age two, I begged my mother to take me to Sunday School. (At that time, she was taking Mabel and Eileen by streetcar to the Metropolitan Tabernacle). When she said, "I'll take you when you get a little bigger," I got up on a chair and said, "I bigger now, Mommy!"

I read I could string beads when I was two and a half years old. When I was three I could bounce a ball and catch it six times without missing, and I had memorized Psalm twenty-three by heart.

My first memory is when I was five years old and we were living on St. Charles Street in Vancouver, B.C., Canada. I was on the front porch. I remember stairs. Lots of stairs! My sister Eileen, three and a half years my senior, and my older sister Mabel, eighteen months older than Eileen, were there with me. Shirley must have been in the house as she would be only a little over a year old.

For some reason, Eileen dared me to jump off the high porch from the high ledge by the window! Unfortunately, I landed with my tongue out, my chin hit my knee, and my teeth chomped down on my tongue almost severing it.

My next memory is sitting on my mother's lap in a rocking chair, my tongue wrapped with a strip torn from an old white sheet. I can still feel how awful that felt. And I still have a slit in my tongue to prove that this really happened.

Infamous stairs!
Front: Mabel, Shirley, Norma.
Back: Mama, Eileen

There's another memory from my fifth year of life. In 1936, our whole family, other than my dad and me, came down with Scarlet Fever. Dad was relegated to the basement so he could still go out to try to find work (this was during the Great Depression), our house was quarantined, and I somehow survived trying to help look after my very sick mother and sisters. About the only thing I remember about that was climbing up on the counter to pour out bowls of cereal for them all. And I do remember that my sisters had what they called "running

. . . .

ears" (ear infections) that caused them hearing problems later in life. And then I came down with Scarlet Fever, but by then Mother was better and could look after me.

In 1937, in the middle of my first grade, we moved into a house my dad built, but I'm getting ahead of my story. I need to go back to my forbears, of whom, unfortunately, I know very little, but I will at least try to give a little background. I'm sure my sisters have different memories than mine, but I will share what I remember as accurately as I possibly can.

The summer before my mother passed away in 1982, I decided this was the time to get a history of my parents' lives. I arrived in Maple Ridge, B.C., Canada from Santa Ana, California armed with a tape recorder and many blank tapes to accomplish my goal. Sadly, however, my father refused to give me permission. Fortunately, my mother did write down a few details from her life, and from her notes I will begin my story.

2

Hilda Otto

My mother was christened Huldah but was known as Hilda for most of her life. She was born on July 20, 1902 in Minsk, Volinia, Russia to August and Amelia (nee Streich) Otto. Since I never met my grandfather, I know very little about him. My grandparents had separated long before I met my grandmother. Interestingly, on the Internet there is a 38-page genealogy of Krzysztof Otto, my Great Grandfather. It lists that my German grandparents were born in Poland. At some point they moved to Russia where my mother was born.

Then in 1904, August moved to a little farm outside Morris, Manitoba, Canada. A year later, Amelia, my mother Hilda and her two older siblings, Matilda (Tillie) and Charles (Charlie), joined him. My mother always told me she was a baby when she came over, but according to this genealogy, she would have been around two.

On the ship coming over from Europe, one of the passengers noticed Hilda, a pretty child, and approached Amelia to see if she'd be willing to let him adopt her as his own. "I guess he noticed our clothing was old and tattered," said Hilda. "He knew we were poor and thought money would be welcome."

"I'll give you one thousand dollars," said the man. Amelia refused, and for the rest of the trip she lived in fear he might try to kidnap Hilda.

Those early days in Canada were hard as they often lacked food. In fact, one day there was absolutely no food in the house. Distressed, Amelia just sat there crying. Enter a Mr. Karlinsky.

"My goodness," he said, "what's the matter?"

"There's nothing in the house to eat,'" said Amelia.

"In this land of plenty?" said Mr. Karlinsky. He immediately left without another word and returned shortly with a load of groceries that included flour, potatoes and sugar.

One day August and Amelia were out working in the field. Hilda, about four, was in the house with her brother Charlie. Ever curious, she pulled a pan of boiling hot water off the stove over her head and down the whole right side of her body. Charlie quickly ran out and got his parents, but by the time they got into the house, Hilda's clothes were stuck to her body. When Amelia pulled off Hilda's clothes, her skin came off with it.

They couldn't afford a doctor so they did what they could. They brought in white puffballs from the fields, dried them on the stove, and then applied them to the burned parts of Hilda's skin. Then Amelia wrapped Hilda's arm in a sling. Later, when she took off the bandage, Hilda couldn't straighten her arm. The loose scalded skin had grown together. There was only one thing to do. Amelia put Hilda's arm on her knee and broke open the skin with a pop. It was crude, but it saved Hilda an operation. Ever after she had a little webbing of

. . . .

skin in the crux of her arm. Her eyes were also closed for several days, but thankfully no harm was done to them.

As Hilda healed, there was another problem. Whenever she combed her hair, it fell out by the handful where the hot water had scalded her on the right side of her head. At age six when she started school, her hair had to be pulled over to cover her bald spot. Often, when the wind blew her hair, her bald spot was exposed. Some children would make fun of her and call her "Baldy." During her younger days, this disfigurement caused her a lot of pain. As an adult, however, she often thanked God for the wonderful way He had spared her life. Hilda suffered no ill effects from the burn, though for years her head was tender.

One after another, children began to come into the Otto household, and before long, August and Amelia had ten children. Grandma actually bore 17 children, but only the ten survived. The genealogy lists three infants died before Tillie was born in 1896 and four more after Lydia (Emily) who was born in 1916.

With a large family, it was obvious they needed a larger house. They found one in the town of Morris, Manitoba, a few miles outside the larger city of Winnipeg. This enabled Amelia to get work outside the home to help support the family.

One night in the cold winter of 1911, a fire broke out and in no time the house was engulfed in flames. August scurried around getting all the children out, plus two boarders. He thought everyone was safe, but then asked, "Where's Huldah?" Without waiting for an answer, he rushed up the stairs, endangering his life, and found her in her burning bed almost suffocated by the smoke. He scooped her up and fled down the stairs to safety, the stairs burning and collapsing behind them. Hilda's comment in later years was, "I was nine years old, and again our wonderful Lord spared me. Our house burned to the ground along with all our worldly possessions but the people of Morris were truly wonderful. They gave us furniture along with clothing and we were able to set up housekeeping again, this time renovating our barn into a home. The chimney would never have passed inspection, but they didn't have any fire regulations in those days. We had many fires in that home but we always managed to *blow* them out."

The Otto Family in 1912: L.to R.: Samuel, August (father) Charlie, Tillie, Hilda (10), Amelia (mother), Ed (on lap). In front: Harry, Elsie.
Not pictured: Olga, Emily, Adeline

One day after Hilda had cleaned the house from top to bottom, she made a cup of tea for her mother and herself. All of a sudden they noticed fire coming down the stairway. Hilda rushed out first to a nearby neighbor where her father and men from surrounding areas were visiting. They all came over and put out the fire while she ran over to a distant neighbor to call for the Morris Fire Brigade. She remembers her ears froze that day as she ran out without a hat. The fire engine never made it to the fire. It got stuck in the snow two blocks away, so the firemen came on foot the rest of the way to "see how the fire was doing!"

"Good thing there were always lots of men around in the winter," Hilda added. "It was such a bitter, cold climate not many of them worked in the winter."

After this fire in 1917, August decided to build a new house. Hilda, at 15, did her share of building as well. She built shelves in the pantry and in the basement for fruit storage, and she made the windowsills wider. Their family needed a bigger table, so she built an extension for it. And then she built herself a vanity (dresser) out of apple boxes and scraps of wood. She even whittled a handle for a drawer she made, then painted and dressed it up and used it as a good piece of furniture in her bedroom until she got married.

"I took it with me when I moved out," Hilda said, "although Harry and I used it as a washstand then. And when we moved to British Columbia in 1926, I took my beloved piece of furniture with me. However, in 1928, when we moved back to Manitoba, I sold it to my neighbor and good friend, Mrs. Bessie Airth, for twenty-five cents.

She later discarded it for firewood, so that was the end of all my hard labor."

As an aside, I used to think I got my dexterity in repairing, mending and tackling other household problems from my father. But after reading the above account, I realize I have my mother to thank as well for being such a good "fixer."

Hilda was only able to complete the tenth grade. By then she had to play the role of mother to her brothers and sisters as Amelia worked away from home during the day. Adeline and Emily, Hilda's two younger sisters whom she looked after from birth (and whom Amelia delivered herself and got out of bed the next day to go back to work), called her "Mother." But that got to be too confusing so they decided that Hilda, only 16, should be called, "Grandma." I can't help but wonder why they couldn't call her by her name. Perhaps calling her Grandma gave her some authority when Amelia wasn't around!

In the summer months, along with babysitting and housekeeping, Hilda would take her younger brothers and sisters to pick the wild fruits of the season--strawberries, raspberries, plums, choke cherries, Saskatoons, hazel nuts and cranberries. It was hard, tedious work. They often had to walk five miles to find, pick and clean the berries and nuts. Then they would have to carry their full pails on the long walk back home.

"The very nicest experience I can remember about these berry picking expeditions," recalled Hilda, "is when we ate our lunch. That's one thing that was carefully attended to. It was a nice, big lunch with sweetened cold tea to go with it and we didn't mind carrying it along with us all morning as we picked. No matter how far we had to

. . . .

walk, we always found a beautiful shady spot with lots of trees to eat our lunch. As long as we could sit and rest awhile, we would not tire. We called one such place, 'Paradise.' It had only a few trees off by themselves, but we thought it was wonderful!"

Each summer, she, and her brothers and sisters, passed by the home of a Mrs. Turner. One day Mrs. Turner invited them all in for a brief rest and glass of milk. "It refreshed us greatly," said Hilda, "but then she asked my mother if she could adopt me as she had no children of her own." Yes, a second time in her life, someone wanted to adopt Hilda. Amelia, of course, said, "No!" but that was the end of their refreshing rests and glasses of milk. After that, Mrs. Turner wanted nothing more to do with the children.

(This brings to mind how a Mr. Andrew Bell, who had no children of his own, wanted to adopt me when I was a child of about six or seven. I would be with my mother and sisters at Main St. Gospel Hall and he thought I must be a neighbor girl as he thought I didn't looked like the rest of my family. He was disappointed when my mother pointed out I was her own daughter and I wasn't up for adoption. He later adopted two children of his own. The daughter, Dorothy, became a good friend. I loved to go to the Bell's house to play as they had a wonderful playhouse in the basement of their lovely big home.)

The berries the Otto children picked were used for their own consumption as well as to sell in order to buy enough sugar to preserve berries for themselves. Hilda's older sister Tilly had married at an early age, but there were still eleven Ottos at home.

. . . .

In 1919, when Hilda was 17, she was still picking berries. Near the end of the season she asked her mother if she could use some of the money they got from selling berries to buy a new winter coat. Up until that time, she only had hand-me-downs from their wealthier friends. Her mother agreed. Many years later Hilda said, "I still remember that nice dark green store-bought coat. It made me so happy."

Hilda also helped during threshing time by cooking for a crew of men. Then in the spring of 1920, a store opened in Morris. The first! The owner was Al Laurie, Hilda's girlfriend's brother, and he asked if she'd work for him. Amelia agreed and Hilda happily went to work for $15.00 per week.

That winter Hilda had enough money to take music lessons from the Lutheran pastor's wife, Mrs. Mohr. The lessons cost 75 cents for a half hour, but after only four lessons, her money was needed elsewhere to help the family. She loved music and was happy later to be the church organist, often playing using only one hand!

It was about this time that Hilda had a deep desire to become a Christian but never told anyone, not even her mother. She recalled, "At nine years of age, the Spirit of God began to work in my little heart, for I would make up my mind to be a real good girl in the morning, but before long, I would go down in failure. Now, at age 18, I would often cry on my knees asking God to save me.

"I attended a Mennonite Brethren church. One Sunday evening as I was going out the door, a missionary named, Anna Thiessan, asked me, 'Are you a Christian?' I said, 'No.' She then asked if she could visit me. She faithfully did, but I didn't seem to understand what she was talking about. She gave me my first Bible and along with reading Westerns, I read a chapter from it nearly every night, but I hid the Bible in the bottom of the trunk because I didn't want anyone to see I had it."

A year later, in 1921, the church had special meetings. Hilda was still working at the store, and as her shifts allowed, she attended all the meetings she could.

"I never did learn to dance," said Hilda. "In fact, I thought dancing was just silly jumping around with a man. And I never played cards, nor desired to do so. But there were two things I greatly loved in the world. One was to attend picture shows, and the other was to read storybooks, especially Westerns. Sometimes I would sit up reading until 2:00 a.m. This always annoyed Mother, as I had to get up early in the summer months. On a real busy day I was up at 4:30 and before breakfast, started the duties of the day.

"This particular winter evening, I was reading a Western at the kitchen table when I glanced over at my mother's open Bible. For some reason, I became frightened and rushed up to bed. I began to dream I was still at the table reading my Western when all of a sudden a voice over my shoulder said, 'Do not read this book. Read the Bible.' In my dream I awakened and there was the Bible open in my lap. I then dreamed I was going down, down, down into Hell. In my dream I tried to wake up, and thankfully I did before I actually went all the way down. I still didn't get too alarmed and got up in the morning to do my cleaning chores in the house before going to work."

That morning Amelia was visiting with a neighbor and as Hilda passed by them, she said, "Are you talking about me?"

. . . .

"Yes, we are," said Amelia.

"What about?" asked Hilda.

To her surprise, Amelia said, "I dreamed last night you wanted to be saved."

That struck Hilda like a thunderbolt, but she went merrily on her way, not letting on she was interested. After work that night, she again went to the special church services. Later she couldn't recall what the preacher said except for one verse. Luke 17:34: "One shall be taken; the other left." No matter where she was, the verse kept ringing in her ears. "I was supposed to be serving the public," said Hilda, "but my mind was not on my work. I knew who would be left behind for judgment. Me."

A few days later, after Hilda had cleaned the house and was sweeping dust and dirt into a dustpan, she began to

Hilda, 19 years old, 1921

cry. This was something no one had ever seen her do. Amelia was surprised. "What's the matter?" she said.

"I want to be saved but I don't know how," Hilda replied. Amelia put her arm around her and together they knelt down and prayed. "Now," said Amelia, "tonight when you go to church, you pray."

"I think that night was the last night of the series of meetings," said Hilda "and when I prayed to accept Christ, Mr. Roth, the preacher, rejoiced

. . . .

because I was the first young person in our congregation to express a desire to know the Lord."

That was a happy time for Hilda as many people in the church came to the house to visit and pray with her. "In fact," said Hilda, "we had so much prayer going on in our home, my little sisters, prayed earnestly for the Lord to forgive them and even my brothers prayed."

In the next few weeks, Hilda struggled with doubts about the reality of her salvation, and one night after much prayer and reading of God's Word, she went to bed. It was then she heard an inner voice say, "Truly thy sins are forgiven thee." And she not only heard it once but three times! At that point she jumped out of bed and ran into her mother's bedroom and said, "I believe I am saved." This was March 1, 1921, and in her own words, "That was the greatest experience I ever had in all my nearly nineteen years!"

The days that followed were full of joy and thanksgiving that her load of sin was gone. She couldn't stop praising the Lord, and the Bible she had been ashamed to have people see her read, became her most important book, and for that matter, the only book she read. Gone was her desire to read Westerns and she would tell anyone who would listen that she was a "born again Christian."

This became a real problem at work. When she tried to tell her boss, Al Laurie, what had happened to her, he would say, "You're crazy!" She didn't know how to answer, but she finally said, "Yes, I guess you will have to be crazy, too, if you want to get to Heaven." This was too much for Mr. Laurie. "You are spoiling my business," he said. "I'm sorry, but you're fired."

"This saddened me," said Hilda, "for I liked my work. I felt selling was my line. I thought that when I told people about this wonderful salvation, they would all want it immediately. But it was not so. All the people who knew me in that little town of Morris agreed with Mr. Laurie. They all thought I was crazy. I lost all my friends except for a Catholic girlfriend, Laura Jerome. She wrote me a lovely letter and in it she said she would still be my friend and wished she could say her sins were all forgiven. For ten years we were great friends until one day, after I was married and living in Vancouver, I sent her a salvation tract. I never heard from her again even though I begged her again and again in letters to write."

Hilda longed for a Christian girlfriend and kept asking God to bring another young person in her church to Himself. In the meantime, she started a youth meeting and a few of her non-Christian friends came. "Some only came once," she said. "They said it was too boring. They thought we would play games, but I wanted to read God's precious Word, sing many hymns and pray. Fortunately a few others kept coming and within a year, not just one came to Christ, but eight young people were saved by God's wonderful grace."

One of these, Tilly Jaster, became a dear friend. They had many precious times together speaking about the things of God. Tilly had a wonderful soprano voice, and Hilda sang alto, so together they sang numberless duets in church, accompanied by Hilda playing the organ.

With the joy of the Lord in their hearts, these nine young people would go from house to house reading God's

Word, singing and praying with all who would invite them in, and they also had many home prayer meetings. Then in 1923, a special preacher arrived to hold Gospel meetings. His name was Rev. J.S. Domm, and from the very first night of the meetings it was evident the Holy Spirit was working in the hearts of those who came. One of the first to come forward for salvation was Hilda's younger sister, Elsie. "About 60 people expressed their faith in Christ during those special meetings," said Hilda. "What a wonderful sight to see all those young people come forward!"

With so many young people, Hilda decided to start a choir. For three years she had a handsome young man by the name of Harry Van Boeyen come faithfully every week

for practice. "I fell in love with him," said Hilda, "and we were married on Friday, October 30, 1925."

The irony of this is that Harry never went to church again except for weddings and funerals and this became a lifelong source of tension and disharmony in the home.

And now that Harry, my father, has been introduced, I want to move on to share a little about him. As mentioned in Chapter 1, because Hugh and I were authors, my dad was not too forthcoming with his history. I do remember him telling me our name, "Van Boeyen," meant "from the handcuff." Perhaps he found some horse thieves in his background and decided to end his investigation right then and there! We'll never know. I hope he was joking!

3

Harry Van Boeyen

When Harry (christened Harman) came into Hilda's life, she had a relationship with him for three years, but she didn't talk to him about his faith or pray with him. This is interesting because it was her practice with many others. Over the years she often talked about how she felt God calling her to be a missionary. Harry, however, was such a charmer, he swept her off her feet and all thoughts about the mission field were far from her mind. In the following difficult years with him, she would often think of that call she ignored and wondered more than once if perhaps she had missed God's best for her life.

Harry, the oldest of seven sons born to Herman and Wiempje (nee Van Twillert) Van Boeyen, was born on March 7, 1902 in Bunskoten, Holland. The Van Boeyen family made and sold cane chairs. When Great Grandma Van Twillert remarried a Mr. Kelderman after her first husband died, he owned a four-story mill and that became Wiempje's home. One of the few stories we know about the mill is that one day lightning struck, and although there was no fire, the horses were killed and all the exposed nails turned blue!

Since horses were the major form of transportation in Harry's early years, they held vivid memories for him. He remembered visiting his grandparents in Holland and how they had to cross a big ditch and dike to get there. One particularly vicious horse would always bite. On one occasion, the horse picked up Harry with his teeth and threw him in the air. Harry, in telling this story, also mentioned that we should never say "hello" to anyone riding a horse because the horse only hears "whoa" and stops!

Grandma Van Boeyen's childhood home in Holland

Herman and Wiempje (she was given the name Violet when they came to Canada) were Christians and brought their boys up to honor their mother and father. It was for this reason Harry was willing to work without pay for his father until he was 21. One sad memory he often mentioned was how he had asked his father for a quarter to go to the Fair but his father wouldn't give it to him.

The Herman Van Boeyen family. Back: Henry, Cornelius, Herman, Harry, William, Clarence. Front: Albert, Wiempje (Violet), Johnny

Another memory is his father telling the boys at meal times, where the Bible was read at each meal, "Eat your food, and do your chewing out in the field." Harry often remarked that he felt his father treated his animals better than his sons.

Harry only completed the 6th grade, but he was an intelligent man and didn't let his lack of education stop his learning. He was clever with his hands and could build

and repair whatever machine needed fixing from tractors
to household appliances to cars.

His first job was driving
a six-horse team in Morris,
Manitoba where he
grew up after coming
over from Holland with
his parents at the age of
seven or eight. He
remembers he worked five
months and earned $70.00
plus room and board.

In 1925, at age 23, he
married Hilda Otto and the
next year they moved to
Vancouver. Two years
later they moved back to
Morris, but soon decided
Vancouver had more
opportunities, and moved
back.

The clock on the shelf in
this photo, taken shortly after they were married, was a
wedding gift from Harry's parents. It now sits on a shelf
in my living room!

Hilda and Harry had four daughters: Mabel Inez, born
August 11, 1926, Eileen Vivian, born February 19, 1928,
Norma Isobel, born July 8, 1931 and Shirley Amelia, born
April 9, 1935. The last two were born during the Great
Depression.

· ·

These were very hard years for Harry. He would often start out in the morning, black metal lunch pail in hand, willing to do anything to provide for his family. Some days, although he looked all day, nothing was available. Other days he would make a few dollars digging ditches or tearing down buildings. This no doubt gave him the experience he needed to build his own house in Vancouver in 1937. Later, he was hired by Blaine Boiler Works and was able to obtain his welder papers, one of the first men in Vancouver to do so. His number was in the low twenties! From there he went to work for Gordon Latham Ltd. as a welder and oil burner mechanic. This was a mixed blessing as his younger brother Cornie had married the owner's daughter and was his boss until his early retirement at age 56 in 1958.

Harry then transferred his skills from boiler making to making things grow. While Hilda created a beautiful park-like flower garden on their acre property at 12462-232nd St. in Maple Ridge, B.C., Harry grew bedding plants in greenhouses he built and had great skill in growing ornamental trees. He sold both the trees and bedding plants for many years.

Harry also had many artistic talents. Apparently in his early years of marriage he did several oil paintings, although none of them survived. In his retirement years, he enjoyed polishing rocks, making jewelry, taking photos and developing and printing them and working on his stamp and coin collections. He also enjoyed fishing and traveling with Hilda across Canada and up into the Northwest Territories in a van he outfitted and made into a camper.

As I begin my story, he was a young man of thirty and
although he had grown up in a Christian home, by this
time he was often antagonistic toward Christians and
Christianity, making our divided home unhappy.

4

Early Years
1937-1943

In the first chapter I mention two memories from the year 1936, when I was five years old, and another memory from 1937 when we moved into an unfinished house my dad was building at 7721 Ontario Street in South Vancouver.

I remember, when we moved in we didn't have inside plumbing. There was an outhouse in a shed at the back of the property that also housed rabbits we raised for eating, but often became pets before Dad killed them. I cried many tears over that! There were no cabinets or sink in the kitchen, and only framing for some of the walls. Little by little my dad was able to finish the two-bedroom, one-bath home with living room, kitchen and an upstairs bedroom that became the special domain of my younger sister Shirley and me. There was also a basement that I remember Dad digging out while we were living there. Hugh recalls thirteen years later when we were dating that he also helped my dad dig out more of the basement. I especially remember the steps down to the basement. I tumbled down them more than once!

From 1929 to the beginning of the Second World War we went through the Great Depression. We were poor, but I never felt poor even though we were on Welfare (then

. . . .

called "Relief" in Canada) for ten years. Try as he might, Dad could not find work. It's for this reason our garden was a blessing and help to provide food for the six of us. Every spring my sisters and I had the task of picking up buckets of small rocks and stones out of the soil. It was terrible soil, but somehow it always yielded a crop!   I remember meat was scarce but homegrown vegetables were plentiful. And we seemed to eat a lot of liver. I still like it to this day!

We had a cookie jar that was always full of molasses cookies as   the recipe didn't call for an egg.   Mother "canned" all summer and fall and I can still see the basement shelves that were full of quart bottles of fruit and vegetables, provisions for the winter. My sisters and I helped by shelling peas by the tubful as we sat on the back stairs. It seemed we'd never get them all shelled.

Those back stairs hold many happy memories for me. We had an older cousin, Dorothy Maclean, who was one of the WAVES (Women Accepted for Voluntary Emergency Service) during WWII. When she had her leave, she would come by for a visit, usually bringing gifts!   But what I remember most was how she loved to color with us. We'd sit on one of the rungs of the stairs, our legs dangling through, and use the stair just above as a table.

Cousin Dorothy and Norma coloring on the back steps

My sisters and I would pick our homegrown strawberries and raspberries and those wonderful green and wax (yellow) beans that are still my favorites. It was in that raspberry patch in our back yard that I learned to yodel, but we won't go into that! We also grew potatoes that were stored in the cold basement in bins and seemed to last all winter. And I remember a crock in the dirt basement floor that held fermenting cabbage that miraculously, to me, turned into sauerkraut.

My dad and a neighbor next door, Mr. Green, would work together on their houses. As the Depression came to an end, they also found work wrecking old buildings, but money was scarce. My mother told me that often she would only get $5.00 a week with which to buy groceries and clothes, yet amazingly, she always tithed 50 cents and paid 25 cents each week for piano lessons for sisters Eileen and Mabel. I'm sorry I never asked my mother how it was we had a piano in those hard times.

Mama, as we called her, loved to tell how one time when there was no money to buy milk or meat, she walked into the hall and there, on the floor, were two one dollar bills! No doubt they had fallen from Dad's pocket, but she was sure they had come directly from Heaven! Who's to say?

This reminds me of one of my mother's favorite poems, probably because she knew what it was to go hungry, and this was probably her plea at times. She knew it so well she could say it by heart!

O Give to the Hungry Potatoes

An old lady sat in her old armchair
With wrinkled face and disheveled hair
Longing for nothing but potatoes;

For days and for weeks, her only fare
As she sat there in her old arm chair
Had been nothing but potatoes.

And now they were gone, of bad or good
Not one was left for the old lady's food,
Of these her stock of potatoes;
And she sighed and said, "What shall I do?"
Where shall I send, and to whom shall I go
To get some more potatoes."

And she thought of the Deacon over the way
The Deacon so ready to worship and pray
Whose cellar was full of potatoes;
And she said, "I will send for the Deacon to come;
He'll not much mind to give me some
Of such a store of potatoes."

And the Deacon came over as fast as he could,
Thinking to do the old lady some good,
But never thought once of potatoes.
He asked her directly to tell her chief want,
And she, simple soul, expecting a grant,
Immediately answered, "Potatoes."

But the Deacon's religion went not that way,
He was more accustomed to preach and to pray
Than to give of his hoarded potatoes;
So not hearing, of course, what the old lady said,
He arose to pray with uncovered head,
But she only thought of potatoes.

He prayed for patience, for wisdom, for grace;
But when he prayed, "O Lord, give her peace,"
She audibly sighed, "Give potatoes."
And at the end of each prayer that he said
He heard not an "Amen," but heard instead
The same request for potatoes.

The Deacon was troubled; knew not what to do,
'Twas embarrassing, very, to have her act so
About these carnal potatoes;
So ending his prayer, he started for home
As the door closed behind him,
he heard a deep groan,
"O give to the hungry potatoes."

And the groan followed him all the way home
In the midst of the night it haunted his room,
"O give to the hungry potatoes."
He could bear it no longer; he arose and dressed,
From his well-filled cellar, taking in haste,
A bag of his best potatoes.

Again he went to the widow's lone hut,
Her sleepless eyes, she had not yet shut
As she longed for some potatoes.
So entering in, he poured out on the floor
A bushel or more of his goodly store
Of his very best potatoes.

And when you hear this simple tale,
Pray for the poor and praying, prevail!
Begin your prayers with alms and good deeds,

Search out the poor with their cares and their needs;
Pray for peace, and grace, and heavenly food,
For wisdom, and guidance, for all these are good,
BUT DON'T FORGET THE POTATOES![2]

This wasn't the only poem my mother memorized. She especially enjoyed Annie Johnson Flint's poem, *What God Hath Promised*. It's become a favorite of mine, too.

What God Hath Promised

God hath not promised skies always blue,
Flower-strewn pathways all our lives through;
God hath not promised sun without rain,
Joy without sorrow, peace without pain.

But God hath promised strength for the day,
Rest for the labor, light for the way,
Grace for the trials, help from above,
Unfailing sympathy, undying love.[3]

Mama also memorized whole chapters of Scripture as when she couldn't sleep at night, she'd love to spend those awake hours repeating helpful verses. Later, when she was 80 and nearing the end of her life, it bothered her that she had forgotten so much of what she memorized.

"Not to worry," I assured her. "It's in your *computer* (head) and Jesus said, 'Heaven and earth will pass away, but my words will never pass away.'"[4] That gave her great comfort.

---

[2] John Tyler Pettee (1822-1907)
[3] Annie Johnson Flint (1862-1932)
[4] (Matthew 24:35, NIV).

. . . .

One thing that stands out in my mind from the Depression was how Mama shared what little we had with many unemployed men who would come by asking if they could earn money by working around the yard or house. We didn't have money to pay them, but Mama would ask these unkempt men in for a meal and serve them what she had. Often it was just a couple of fried eggs and toast. I'm not sure we'd do this today, but back in the 40s, it was perfectly safe.

Another precious memory from my childhood is about our neighbors, Stan and Vi Wells, who lived a couple of doors down the back lane. They loved children, although they had none of their own, and would host treasure hunts for all the neighborhood children. They had a large yard and it was such fun to hunt among the bushes, in trees and around rocks. Our treasure may only be a fancy button or some little trinket, but I enjoyed these treasure hunts so much I kept up the tradition with my grandchildren, putting my clues in rhyme and their treasure would be a dollar bill or a chocolate bar for each.

Stan and Vi became very close friends right into my teens and I often thanked God for them. I felt they were a godsend as I could visit them and escape from my often unhappy home. And it's from them I learned to love Country Western music that I had to eschew when I married Hugh. He hated that music. He would always say the vocalists sounded like "dying ducks." Interestingly, however, we found out later, when he was doing his own memoirs, he had liked it when he was young!

. . . .

One New Year's Eve when I was 16 or 17, I decided to see the old year out and the New Year in with my sister Eileen. At the stroke of midnight, Eileen and I went out on the back porch and saw Stan and Vi out on their porch and we yelled, "Happy New Year!" This woke up my dad and in a rage he came at me to strike me. I tried to get upstairs to my bedroom but he kicked me all the way up the stairs and when I got to my bed, I rolled underneath it to escape his wrath. I never understood why he got so angry at times. Thinking back, it may have been that he worked so hard during the day, having his sleep disturbed would make him tired for his work the next day. This, of course, is no excuse for his lack of anger management, but it helps me not to think too unkindly about him!

I went to John Wesley Sexsmith School just two blocks from my home for Grades One to Eight, as we say in Canadienese! There was one class for each grade. I remember my first grade teacher was Miss Rowntree. Miss Partequin, a huge woman, was the second grade teacher and she was not my favorite. She once put brown sticky tape on my mouth when I was talking too much. At times she'd put children upside down in the wastebasket to get them to behave (not leave them there, of course, but just to scare them). Miss Main was my third and fifth grade teacher and I especially remember my East Indian 8th grade teacher who took a special interest in me and wrote Mother once to say that I was too thin and she should feed me more. I guess at that time I was ten pounds underweight. (Oh, to have that problem now!) Mama sent back a note to tell him to stick to his teaching and let her worry about that! He once sent me out of the room when I was acting up in class. I remember I put my foot in the door so he couldn't shut it. I told him I'd be good, and he let me back in.

The only other time I got in trouble in school was when I said, "Whiskey!" in a loud sneeze. That was how my dad sneezed and I didn't think anything about it. I believe I got a detention for that!

Back to John Wesley Sexsmith School, the basement was our gym. We also had an auditorium where we had assemblies and put on many concerts. I saw my first movie there. It was *Gunga Din.* I loved to act in plays and in 7th grade I was in two dance numbers. One was the Sailor's Hornpipe when we all wore sailor suits and hats. The other was a rhythm dance with rubber balls and we all wore pastel satin short dresses with a flared skirt, something like the photo to the right. I don't remember what this patriotic getup was all about! I think I was eight at the time.

When I was in the third grade, our class field trip was to go downtown and see a magician. Mama thought this was "of the devil" so I was told I'd have to spend the day in the second grade with the evil Miss Partequin. Mama took pity on me and said I didn't have to do that and she'd take me on a trip to see her good friend Bessie Airth. Off we went on the

Interurban tram we caught at the foot of our street which was a good ten blocks away. Today Burnaby is considered a suburb of Vancouver and is only about fifteen minutes away from the center of town. However, to get there in 1939 it was considered a major trip. During the Great Depression, the Airth family was even worse off than we were. They lived in a ramshackle abandoned building that once housed a store and post office. It was great fun to explore the abandoned part of the house they didn't use.

The Airths had a goat and I was served goat milk for lunch. I took one sip and couldn't drink another drop. All I can say is, "Ugh!" A money-saving hint my mother learned that day from Mrs. Airth was to use baking soda instead of toothpaste for our teeth. I was glad when there was money again for toothpaste!

I did well in elementary school. I always ranked first or second. My rival was Larry Yick, a Chinese boy who often walked home from school with me. He lived at the bottom of Ontario Street on the other side of Marine Drive where the Chinese grew their produce gardens. But it was a friendly rivalry even when we tried to outdo each other.

Another memory I have of those Depression years is that we could only have one pair of shoes. They were called "Oxfords," plain black shoes with laces. We had to have them soled three times before we were issued a coupon to get a new pair. I remember Mama kneeling on the floor on Saturday nights in front of the kitchen stove (in which we burned sawdust in a hopper), newspapers spread out on the linoleum floor and five pair of shoes lined up for her to polish for Sunday church.

When Dad finally got work and Mama had a bit of spending money, she took Shirley and me shopping. Some black patent Sunday shoes for Shirley and me were the first items on her list! That winter we also got red coats with fur collars, and in the spring, Mama bought me a rose suit and Shirley a pale blue one. Up until then we were receiving used clothes from the school nurse. One winter my mother made me a coarse brown tweed jumper out of an old overcoat. I wore that jumper all winter with the only two blouses I had. When one was in the wash, I'd wear the other one! In the spring mother bought me a flowered dirndl skirt (a full tiered skirt with a tight waistband) and a white peasant blouse. I remember twirling around in that skirt feeling so light and free!

After WWII, 1945. With cousin Dorothy Maclean
(second from left) between sister Shirley (10) and Norma (14)
in their new suits. Sister Eileen (17 ½) on the right

Church was very important to my mother and she certainly taught us not to "neglect the assembling of ourselves together." It was a bone of contention with my

. . . .

dad that she was always going to church. And he could never understand why Mama wanted to give money to the church when we had so little, but she firmly believed the first ten-percent belonged to God. This was the cause of many arguments. And because Mother felt Sunday was to be kept holy, she was very strict about not letting us cut with scissors, read comics, listen to the radio or even use crayons in our coloring books. We stayed in our Sunday best and went to church in the morning, Sunday School at 2:00 p.m. and evening service at 7:00 p.m. Need I say, I wasn't too fond of Sundays!

Because she didn't drive, we walked to Main Street Gospel Hall (Plymouth Brethren) only a couple of blocks away. The worst part about going to Sunday School on Sunday afternoons was having to walk past our neighbor's house. That's where Jimmy Biles lived and his father was my dad's boss at Blaine Boiler Works. I think this made him feel superior and he would especially feel he could lord it over me. He called me "Goody Two Shoes," "Norma Van Bum," and "Norma Stinker-boin." And he'd chant, "Norma Van Boeyen loves Stanley Boon," (a boy who never washed his hair and was always in trouble at school.) I remember those days as "miserable."

My one friend at the Gospel Hall was Norma Campbell (later married to Jim Smith). It was magical for me to go to her home with a book-lined study and several rooms filled with lovely furniture. When I was nine we went to Burrard Inlet Bible Camp together. One day our counselor got all us girls together and asked us if we wanted to ask Jesus into our hearts. Because everyone said, "Yes," I did, too, but when we prayed, I didn't feel I was really ready to do this, and later when I was older I knew I was not ready to meet Jesus.

My other good friend was Jean Barr who lived a distance away in New Westminster. She also went to a Brethren Assembly. I gave her the nickname, "Bean Jar." I can't remember how we became friends but I liked her so much, I gave Wendy "Jean" as her middle name. (She later dropped it and became "Wendy Steven Asimakoupoulos" after she was married.)

My best friend at school was Florence Baker, who was also on Welfare, and since she lived only a block and a half away, we were bosom buddies. To this day we still exchange Christmas cards. There was an empty lot across the street from her house and every night in the summer months, all the neighborhood children would gather for Scrub Baseball. When it was time for us to go home, we would hear our mother calling our names. Another interesting tidbit is that when friends came by to play, they never knocked on the door. They just stood at the bottom of the stairs and called for us.

In this same vacant lot we had fun climbing the trees. Someone had pounded nails into a tree trunk to make it easier. One day Shirley put on a new sweater and off we went to play in the vacant lot. She climbed a tree and on the way down she caught her sleeve on one of the nails. She pulled and pulled so hard, the whole sleeve came off! Now she had to go home and tell Mama what happened. This was hard as new clothes were still hard to come by.

"What happened?" asked Mama, rather firmly.

Without batting an eye, Shirley said, "Oh, I just went by a tree and my sleeve fell off."

. . . .

Mama told me years later that she thought that was the cutest excuse she ever heard and had to turn away so Shirley wouldn't see her smiling. I guess the punishment Shirley received was that she had to wear the sweater with the sleeve clearly sewn on!

Florence and I, while we were "good" girls, could also get into mischief. One day, when we were ten or eleven, we decided to walk to the Fraser River, a couple of miles from our homes. We had been warned never to go there, but go we did on a beautiful, sunny, hot summer day when there was nothing else to do. Often there was nothing more to do than lie on our backs and gaze up at the sky and see who could find the most interesting shapes in the cloud formations. But this day we wanted a bit of excitement. And we were not disappointed!

When we got to the river, we went out on a half-submerged log that extended into the river. We had no idea how deep it was at the end of the log, but there we were, balancing on it, and the inevitable happened. We fell in! Fortunately the cold water was only chest high and we quickly got ourselves onto the shore. I shudder to think if it had been over our heads. At that time, I could not swim.

Now we had a problem. How were we to get home with our wet clothes and not let our parents know we had disobeyed? I don't know if it was Florence's idea or mine, but we decided to take off our clothes, except for our slips, and hang them on the nearby bushes to dry. (Girls didn't wear slacks or shorts in those days. We were always dressed in either a skirt and blouse or dress...with a slip!) No one was around, so we felt on this hot day our dresses and panties would quickly dry and no one would be the wiser.

We were having a great time as we played tag and sat for a while on the bank and just talked.

"How's your tan coming?" Florence asked. Getting a good tan was our goal in the few good sunny days we had in the Pacific Northwest.

"Great!" I said. "Do you want to see my back?"

"Sure," said Florence.

At the moment I pulled up my slip to show off my tanned back, exposing my bare bottom in the process, we heard a "wolf whistle." Unknown to us, two boys were hiding behind some bushes watching our whole escapade.

We screamed at the top of our lungs, scaring the boys away, and we quickly put on our damp clothes and began our long trek home. Fortunately our clothes dried by the time we got home. Since our parents have passed away, we can now tell our story without fear of retribution!

I did have a boyfriend when I was twelve—my first. His name was Buddy McLennan. He came to Sexsmith School in the 7th Grade and sat across from me. It was puppy love at first sight for both of us and wonder of wonders, he soon became our paper boy. When he'd arrive with the paper, I'd dash down to the gate and there we'd stand chatting away (for the life of me I can't imagine what we talked about) for at least a half hour while people waited for their papers to be delivered. Our relationship ended when he moved away at the end of 7th grade.

I believe my experience of the Great Depression and poverty in general was a great blessing. It made me more grateful for all the blessings I have today and more aware of the poor and their needs. I'm grateful to my mother for always making me feel I had worth and that being poor was nothing for which I should feel shame. She lived through that difficult period with dignity and thankfulness and came out on the other side with a joyful, giving spirit. Sadly, my father became bitter and resentful for the rest of his life.

There was one painful incident when I was eleven that would forever change our intact, if somewhat dysfunctional, family. My oldest sister Mabel ran away from home. She had just turned sixteen.

Back: Norma, Mama, Shirley
Front: Mabel, Eileen

5

Teens
1944–1949

I n September 1943, my father made Mabel quit school
to get a job. She started as a messenger girl, riding a
bike   in   downtown   Vancouver   to   deliver
correspondence, notices and messages between businesses.
She then moved on to be a receptionist at Radio Station
CKWX. She dated several young men, none of whom my
dad approved, and then began a steady relationship with a
young soldier.

One night he brought her home at midnight and my dad
in anger, kicked the young man down the stairs, told him
not to come back. He then beat Mabel.

When she got to know Bill Reid, an announcer at
CKWX, and told him what life was like at home, he
suggested she go to live with his mother, Mrs. S.L. Reid,
whom everyone called "Mater."

Since I was only eleven when all this happened and not
fully aware of all that was going on, I don't have all the
details. However, I do know that because Mabel was a
minor, she had to appear in court to be granted permission
to stay at Mater's, and later to have permission to marry
Bill. My father was ordered "not to molest or annoy her"
and Mabel won the right to live with Mater "until definite

. . . .

permanent arrangements can be made on her behalf."
Interestingly, this painful incident made my dad more
lenient toward Eileen, a year and a half younger than
Mabel, when she dated Norman McCurrie (whom she later
married). No matter how late she'd get in after a date, he
never said a word.

I don't know the date of Mabel's wedding. None of us
were there. I do know it broke my mother's heart.

For many years Mabel couldn't come home with Bill as
my Dad was prejudiced against Indians (Bill was half
Haida, half Scottish) and went on to become Canada's
foremost Indian artist and carver. His pieces are in the
University of British Columbia Museum, the Provincial
Museum in Victoria, B.C., the Vancouver, B.C. Airport and
in front of the Canadian Embassy in Washington, D.C.).
Mother would meet Mabel in a neutral place to have a visit
with her. Eleven years later, however, when Mabel and
Bill divorced and she married a full Haida Indian, Billy
Stevens, my dad's attitude had softened and a strong
relationship with them developed.

World War II began in 1939 and the Great Depression
ended. Dad was finally able to get a job, we got off
"Relief" and life in many ways, became much happier in
the Van Boeyen household.

The war affected us by the rationing of gas and food
products. All of us were issued ration books, but with our
large vegetable garden, not only in our back yard, but also
on a lot across the lane that was our "Victory Garden," we
managed to eat well. I still remember the practice air raid
warnings, blackening our windows by pulling down the
shades or covering them with black curtains, and a sign on

. . . .

all the streetcars that said, "Sorry, Sir, sugar shortage situation serious!"

We had many ways to help with the war effort by collecting newspapers, pieces of tin foil, bacon fat, toothpaste tubes (made of soft metal) and string. I was fourteen when the war ended in 1945, and I can remember the big bold headlines in the newspaper and great celebrations in downtown Vancouver.

My father at this time was not a Canadian citizen so was not called up to go to war. However, I do remember how upset he was when the Dutch government tried to get him to enlist in the Dutch army. And not just once, but several times. We found out later, after he passed away, that he didn't get his Canadian citizenship until 1955.

A year before the war ended, when I was in the 7th grade, a Mr. Herb Harris came to Main Street Gospel Hall to hold a series of "Gospel" (evangelistic) meetings. Every night for six weeks, I went with Mama. Mr. Harris, a hell-fire and brimstone preacher, really got to me one night when he thundered from his reading of Revelation 21:27, "Is your name written in the Lamb's Book of Life?" That night when we got home, I told my mother I didn't think my name was in that Book.

"Oh, Norma," said Mama, "don't you remember when you were at Burrard Inlet Bible Camp you told me you had prayed and asked Jesus into your heart?"

"No, Mama," I insisted. "I just prayed that prayer because everyone else did."

We talked for a while about this and the more I protested I was not "saved," the more Mama insisted I was, and because it was so late, she finally told me to go to bed.

In the morning, I was still troubled about whether or not I was on my way to Heaven, so I called downstairs and said, "Mom, I can't go to school today. I've got to get right with God!" Amazingly she let me stay home.

I got out my King James Bible, knelt down by my bed and opened to Romans 10, verse 9: "If thou shalt confess with thy mouth the Lord Jesus and shalt believe in thine heart that God hath raised him from the dead, thou shalt be saved." As I read this over and over, I kept crying out to God to save me. Finally, I looked at the verse again. "I do confess that You are Lord, Jesus," I said out loud. "And I do believe God raised You from the dead..." It was like a light bulb came on in my head! "Oh, in order to do that, You first had to die , didn't you? I see! I see! I do believe You died for me!"

It was as simple as that. In a moment I knew the next phrase was true for me: "You shall be saved."

I dashed down the stairs to tell Mom the good news, and we rejoiced together.

I was almost as enthusiastic as my mother telling my friends I was saved. I don't remember any of them calling me crazy, but some weren't as friendly to me after that.

I was anxious that my good friend Florence Baker have what I had, and she agreed to come to the meeting the next night. I even got her to "stay behind," as the Brethren like to say for those seeking salvation, but when one of the elders asked her if she'd like to accept Christ as her personal Savior, she said, "No." We were still good friends after that, but in high school we each found other friends.

A year later, in 1945, I was baptized by immersion and shortly later given a Sunday School class of Jr. High girls that I taught for four years. Up until then, Bill Funston had been my Sunday School teacher and I am grateful for him, my mother's example and God's Word that helped me grow in my faith and knowledge of God.

As an aside, I always jokingly said I was fully "covered" as mother had me baptized as an infant in the United Church of Canada. Later, we attended Metropolitan Tabernacle whose beliefs did not include infant baptism, so she had me dedicated. I had believer's immersion baptism in Main Street Gospel Hall at age 14, and was commissioned for the mission field in Ruth Morton Baptist Church. For a long time I used to say I was a "Bapto-Brethren," but then we attended an English speaking Presbyterian Church in Mexico City, and when we moved stateside, I became an ordained elder in Trinity Presbyterian Church.

I would like to give a statement of my beliefs and practices, just in case the readers of this history wonder what, with this background, I believe!

I believe in the Trinity—Father, Son and Holy Spirit; that Jesus Christ is the only Son of God, that He was conceived by the Holy Spirit and born of the Virgin Mary, was sacrificed for my sin, was bodily raised again the third day and is now seated at the right hand of God interceding for me (Romans 8:34).

I believe that salvation comes through faith in Jesus Christ and is not of works, but good works must accompany faith to demonstrate I belong to Him (Matthew 5:17; 1 Timothy 6:18; Hebrews 10:24; James 2:17,18; 1 Peter 2:12); that baptism is a sign that I belong to Christ and want to walk in newness of life; that meeting together for worship, prayer, fellowship and mutual encouragement is commanded and important, and that all believers have been given spiritual gifts to be used for the building up of the church (1 Corinthians 14:12; Ephesians 2:10).

I believe in the eternal security of the believer, but that it is important to live an examined life and keep short accounts with God, confessing my sins daily and turning away from them with the Holy Spirit's help.

I believe it is important to spend time daily with the Lord in study, prayer, worship and meditation to maintain a growing relationship with Him. I believe Bible memorization is important and practice it. I believe it is important to be pure and holy and obey God's will as He reveals it, no matter the cost, and that it is important to confess my faith to others (Romans 10:10).

I believe I am to reflect Jesus Christ to others at all times and, therefore, in all my words, deeds, actions, appearances and lifestyle, all should be for the display of His splendor and bring glory to His name. In no way do I want to dishonor Him.

I believe God punishes sin wherever it is found and that the unbeliever will spend eternity apart from God in the place He's prepared for them.

I believe that Jesus is coming back again to take me, and all those who believe in Him, to dwell with Him in Heaven for eternity.

Up until the age of 14, I contributed to the finances of our home by babysitting, and strawberry and raspberry picking with my mother in the summers. I gave every cent I made to my mother. Then in the summer of 1946, when I was 15, I worked for the Pro-Made Golf Company making golf clubs. One day while polishing a wood, my long hair got caught up in the polishing machine and yanked a big hunk out of the back right side of my head. Like my mother, I now have a bald spot, much smaller than hers, which I continue to struggle to comb my hair over! All the girl employees had to wear bandanas on their heads after that. Like my berry picking and baby-sitting money, I gave all my money home.

That Christmas I got a job at Woolworth's Five and Dime, and in the summer of 1947, I worked for Copp the Shoe Man. Several members of the Copp family attended Main St. Gospel Hall and one of them must have

Norma at 15

recommended me for the job. I worked Christmas and summers for a couple of years during my high school years and then my homeroom teacher, knowing I had pressure at home to get out and find a job, asked me if I would like a full-time secretarial job with the City health department

With a favorable recommendation from her, I was hired to work at Health Unit #1 in downtown Vancouver in an old building, later torn down, off Victory Square where the Vancouver Technical School is now located. This is where I first met Irene Charles (later married to Dave Brummitt) who is still a very good friend. The office then moved to Cordova Street across from Woodward's Department Store where Hugh worked (once a Vancouver landmark, that building no longer stands).

It was here I became the doctor's secretary, took chest x-rays and developed them. I made $50.00 per week and gave $10.00 weekly to my mother for room and board. Finally I was able to begin saving and buying a few things for my own needs.

I attended John Oliver High School, taking the "Commercial Course" to become a secretary. And then Dad insisted it was time to get out and work. Shirley was the only one able to go on from High School. After she had worked to pay for her own tuition, she went to Multnomah School of the Bible for three years. It was there she fell in love and later married Al Lee whom she had known at Ruth Morton Baptist Church.

All of us were very good students. Eileen skipped grades two and four! I often wonder what we could have become if we had been encouraged to continue our education. But that didn't stop us from continuing to learn throughout our lives. After I married Hugh, he inspired me to read theological books. We took biblical courses together through Northwest Baptist Bible College, and we studied linguistics for service with Wycliffe Bible Translators. I went on to do layout work in Wycliffe's publication office in Mexico City, design covers and become the group librarian, learning the Dewey Decimal System. While in Mexico I also took up oil painting and Spanish guitar, and of course we learned to speak Spanish.

Later, after we came back from the mission field, I studied the Bible with Bible Study Fellowship and became a discussion leader. I taught neighborhood Bible studies, wrote and published four books and many articles and poems, edited Hugh's some 35 books and also did editing for other authors, took part in Hugh's writers' workshops in Alaska, Singapore and Vanuatu, worked two years at age 60 in pastoral care at Granville Chapel, and in my 70s,

. . . .

taught English as a Second Language, among other things, and continued leading Bible studies into my 90s.

I've always wished I could have gone on to college, but I feel I'm a life-long learner and will be until I die!

Back to age 15. This was the year of my first real boyfriend. Why my mother allowed me to go out with someone several years my senior I'll never know. In her wisdom, she didn't stop me. If she had, out of rebellion I probably would have kept up the relationship! After two months, I broke it off and didn't date again until I met Hugh when I was 18.

Shortly before I met Hugh, I had become increasingly upset with the fellowship at Main Street Gospel Hall as there was no youth group, only "gatherings," as they called them, at various homes, where often I was not invited. Someone would call up Eileen, three and a half years older than me, and say the "gathering" was only for those over 18. Yet, Eileen would tell me another girl my same age was there.

When I complained to my mother, she'd say, "It's just that they're afraid you'll steal all the boys!" But it didn't make me feel any better.

My good friend Jean Barr lived about three-quarters of an hour away in New Westminster. We'd get together some weekends, but not that often. During those years I was very lonely for Christian fellowship.

In high school I met Beverly Thomas, a fellow Christian, and she asked me to come to some of her church events at Ruth Morton Baptist Church. The young people had something called a "Singspiration" where they met at various homes after the Sunday evening service for food, fellowship and a good old hymn sing. The night it was at Beverly's home, she invited me to come.

As I was leaving, Beverly said, "Come and meet Hugh Steven." He was a tall, slim, blond, curly-headed, handsome young man, and when we were introduced, he bowed low and said, "Do you hail from the Bronx?" He doesn't remember doing that, but I do, because even though I didn't know what that remark meant, I thought he was the cutest boy I'd ever met!

And then Beverly invited me to their Young People's progressive New Year's dinner party on New Year's Eve, 1949. However, Main St. Gospel Hall was having their first-ever New Year's Eve Service, and Mama thought I should go. But she finally gave in, and off I went with my new navy taffeta, flared-skirt dress emblazoned with little white Scottie dogs.

6

Courtship and Engagement

I met Beverly at her house and we walked a few blocks to the pastor's house where the appetizers were being served. Beverly was in charge of two bags of identical paper hats. When the boys arrived, they took a random hat out of the one bag, the girls out of the other, and whoever had the same hat as you was your partner for the evening.

I reached in and got my hat, put it on and looked for a place to sit. Uncommonly shy and not knowing most who would be coming, I decided to sit on the piano bench, directly across from where Beverly was standing in the hall with the hats.

Several came in, chose their hats, but no one had a match to mine. Then Hugh arrived. He looked into the living room, saw me, and said to Beverly, "Hey, give me the same hat as that girl on the piano bench." She shouldn't have, of course, but she obliged. He put on his hat and came over to greet me.

I don't remember much of what went on that evening. We walked to another couple of houses for the entrée and dessert and ended up at Beverly's for a "Singspiration." All the while Hugh was attentive, funny and charming.

He asked if he could take me home, but I had made arrangements to stay at Beverly's for the night. He then

....

asked for my phone number and I flippantly said, "You can look it up in the phone book," and that's what he did. He called me the following Tuesday to go to the Vancouver Symphony Pop concert and this began a weekly date until we were married, a year and five months later on May 5, 1951.

Our courtship was not always smooth sailing as we were young, headstrong and had doctrinal differences. And it didn't help that my dad didn't like Hugh. He felt he was a "Bible toting religious nut," and at times wouldn't even talk to Hugh.

I remember how embarrassed I was one Sunday when Hugh came home for lunch after church and Dad wouldn't get up off the couch where he was lying down feigning sleep. What was worse, we had brought home our friend Neil McKay. Nevertheless, Dad would not budge and and we all had to sit in the kitchen.

Street photographer photo, 1950

There was one other obstacle that would haunt me and keep me awake at night the first four years of our marriage. It was that Hugh told me he felt called to be a pastor. I told him in no uncertain terms I would never make a pastor's wife and he better forget me. Obviously he didn't and I was left with a guilty conscience that I was keeping him from doing God's will.

However, I knew Hugh was my one and only and I guess he felt the same as he proposed to me on my 19th birthday, July 8, 1950. He had invited me to dinner at the Sylvia Hotel, romantically situated directly across from English Bay. Their restaurant, at that time, was on the top floor with a spectacular view. Unknown to me, or his parents, he had already brought a diamond ring. When he popped the question, I said, "Yes" and he put the engagement ring on my finger.

Flushed with excitement, I showed my ring to my mom and dad the following morning, but my dad quickly deflated me by saying, "Hmphf! Piece of glass!" However, Mama and my sisters were excited for me, especially Eileen who was also engaged and was married six months before me. Dad never helped with any expenses for either Eileen or my wedding and as Mama had used all her savings to give Eileen a wedding, when it was my turn six months later, I paid for almost everything.

Hugh paid for the flowers, but since I had to pay for my wedding dress and veil, the invitations, the printed napkins, wedding reception, my trousseau, "Going-Away" outfit, gifts for my sisters (Eileen was my matron of honor, Shirley my bridesmaid, and my six-year-old cousin Mae deHaan my flower girl), I depleted my bank account. At least we didn't have to rent a reception hall. Our reception would be downstairs at Ruth Morton Baptist Church where we would be married and, as members, there was no charge. However, in those days, because the City didn't let married women work, Hugh inherited a penniless, unemployed bride!

. . . .

Hugh's parents, Dave and Mable Steven, were most supportive, and when Mr. Steven's father, Hugh's Grampa Steven, passed away a few months before our wedding, they offered to sell us his small 20 x 20 foot clap-board house (in which Grampa Steven had housed and sold budgies and other birds that resulted in it being rat-infested from all the feed) for $1500.00. Our payments were not to start until four months after the wedding and would only be $35.00 a month, no interest. Good thing! Hugh, a Jr. Manager in Woodward's Stores, made only $35.00 a week!

But this was a few months away and in the meantime, we could fix up his Grampa's house by putting in a partition between the one large room, making a small living room and a tiny kitchen with cabinets. Our kitchen was so small I joked it was the only kitchen I knew where you could sit at the table, reach the pots on the stove, put dirty dishes in the sink, and blow your nose in the living room.

For heating upstairs we had a black and chrome wood-burning cook stove in the kitchen, and a pot belly stove in the street-level basement in front of which we bathed in a galvanized tub. The only bathroom was a single toilet in an enclosed room in the corner of the basement (no inside steps!).

Hugh built the partition with the help of our friend John Scott from Ruth Morton, a cabinet maker at that time, who also built the kitchen cabinets. John and his girlfriend, Thelma Perkins, whom he married a year after us, also helped with the painting. Hugh often said, "They were angels God sent to help us." He couldn't get over how

· ·

they just showed up and worked along with us until the little house was ready for us to move in.

Our first home on 30th Ave. in Vancouver, B.C., Canada

The months sped by and soon May 5th was looming around the corner. My wedding dress and trousseau were bought, the cake ordered, the caterer hired and the invitations printed. Then one rainy day, on a Wednesday, Hugh's day off, Hugh was putting the finishing touches on the little house when there was a knock at the door.

Hugh answered it and there in the pouring rain a man asked if he was Hugh Steven. "Yes," said Hugh and invited him into the porch out of the rain.

"I've just come from your parents' home," he said, "and your mother told me you are to be married in a few weeks."

Puzzled, Hugh said, "Yes."

"I'm sorry," said the man, "but you cannot get married under the name *Steven*. Your parents never legally adopted you and your last name is *Toderas*."

. . . .

"If your minister marries you under the name Steven," the man continued, "he could lose his license. I know this is a shock for you and I'm sorry this wasn't found out sooner. We were going through some old files at the Children's Aid Society and discovered that your file had never been closed as it should have been when you turned 18." (Hugh was now 20.)

Never to take things quietly, when we next saw the Stevens I confronted them with our dilemma, and not too kindly either. I was really upset and said, "How could you let us go ahead thinking Hugh was adopted by you and his last name was Steven. I don't want to be Mrs. Toderas. That's like being married to someone I don't even know."

For a few days we didn't know what we were going to do. As Hugh was not yet 21, the legal age when he could change his name himself, and it would take six months for adoption papers to go through, it looked like we were going to have to be Mr. & Mrs. Toderas and get new invitations printed. But the Stevens, bless their hearts, were able to hire a lawyer and adoption papers were rushed through just in time for our wedding. The cost of the adoption? Thirty-five dollars!

We were not through with upsets even though this traumatic event was settled. Something else was on the horizon that was probably brewing in my dad's heart for some time. I am reminded of Matthew 12:34-35 where Jesus said, "For out of the overflow of the heart the mouth speaks. The good man brings good things out of the good stored up in him, and the evil man brings evil things out of the evil stored up in him." Truly what my father was about to say was evil.

. . . .

One night, a few days before our wedding, I was in the kitchen with my sister washing the supper dishes when suddenly my father said, with all the venom he could muster, "If you marry Hugh, you will end up a prostitute."

It was so ugly, so unexpected, I hardly knew how to respond. It cut through me like a knife. I had endured strappings from his razor strap, had a wooden ruler broken over my head once and had endured many other abuses, but this was the worst. Out of my anguish and unbelief that he would say such a thing, I yelled, "Liar!"

My dad's face contorted in anger and without a word he got out of the kitchen chair where he was sitting reading the paper. I knew what was coming and I tried to get into the bathroom to lock the door, but I didn't make it. I pressed against the wall and threw up my hands and arms over my face as he pummeled me with his large fists.

After he had vented his anger at what I'm sure he thought was my insolence, he walked away and I ran upstairs to my bedroom, threw myself on my bed and sobbed and sobbed feeling in my heart a deep hatred. And then, in between sobs, I heard an inner voice softly say, "But you have Me."

I knew what I had to do. I dried my eyes, asked God to help me, and walked slowly downstairs and into the kitchen where my dad was back reading his newspaper. I walked up to him and stood beside his chair.

"I'm sorry I called you a liar, Dad," I said.

He didn't say a thing. He just kept reading the paper. I waited, hoping he would say he was sorry for saying such a hateful thing or letting his anger get out of control, but when an apology was not forthcoming, I turned and walked away.

. . . .

It took me a while, but I later learned that when I am insulted, I can make it an opportunity to exhibit the Son of God in my life. Oswald Chambers writes in *My Utmost for His Highest:* "A personal insult becomes an opportunity for us to reveal the incredible sweetness of the Lord Jesus." And in doing so, of course, it's also a way to display God's splendor!

Dad continued to say he wasn't going to give me away right up until almost the time for the wedding ceremony. And the last straw was he wouldn't wash his car to get it ready for me, Mama and my sisters to drive to church for our scheduled wedding at 7:00 p.m. So at 4:30 on the afternoon of my wedding day, just two and a half hours before our ceremony, I washed his car and decorated it with some streamers.

I finally knew Dad would give me away when I saw him dressed in his suit, and I breathed a sigh of relief, praying he would not do anything to embarrass me. And he didn't! No one would ever suspect what I had been through to get to this moment. He was as proud as a peacock and pleasant to everyone he met. I was thankful, but also resentful that he had given me such a hard time. I believe this was the beginning of my difficult journey to even want to forgive him, a battle I would wage for over thirty years.

7

Wedding, Honeymoon, Children and a Call

I remember someone commenting that they had never seen a happier bride. They were surprised I had such a big smile on my face as I walked slowly down the aisle on the arm of my father. I've often thought about that as I was anything but happy during those last couple of months before the wedding with Dad making it so difficult for me. Perhaps I was just happy I was beginning a new life with Hugh!

We had a traditional ceremony with traditional vows. My good friend from childhood, Pat Lindburg, later married to Rev. Carl Friedrich, was our soloist. I had met her summers when my mother would send Shirley and me off to stay with our Aunt Nellie and Uncle Henry out in Albion (now incorporated into Maple Ridge, B.C.) about an hour east of Vancouver. They had four children around our ages and lived on acreage, so it was great fun for us city girls. I think we'd stay at least a month and have such fun in the barn jumping off the loft into a pile of hay, and running out to the train tracks in front of the property where we'd wave at the engineers and passengers. Pat came from the city as well to visit her grandparents in Albion, and with cousins Dorothy, Patricia, Victor and

Marjorie, Shirley and I would have endless fun in the long summer days and evenings of the Pacific Northwest.

My wedding bouquet was crescent-shaped with white gardenias and orchids. The perfume was overwhelming! Rev. Howard Phillips, our beloved pastor, married us, and his wife Irene played the organ. Norman McCurrie, my older sister's husband, was Hugh's Best Man. He really was not a close friend at that time, but Eileen asked Hugh to have him so she could walk down the aisle with him and not have to walk down with one of Hugh's friends she didn't know. As it turned out, over the years Norman became one of Hugh's very best friends, so it was a good choice. Neil McKay, Hugh's friend from Young People's (Youth Group) was his other groomsman.

L. to R.: Neil McKay, Norman McCurrie, Hugh, Norma,
Eileen (Van Boeyen) McCurrie, Shirley (Van Boeyen) Lee.
Front Mae (deHaan) Meller

. . . .

Our reception with about 250 people was in Ruth Morton Baptist's basement Sunday School auditorium called John Morton Hall. And I remember we forgot to bring our printed wedding napkins. We used them for years afterwards!

As was the custom in 1951, I left to go back home and change into my "Going Away Outfit" that consisted of a navy gabardine suit, navy straw hat with a veil and small red flowers at the back, an off-white car coat, and red leather shoes and purse. We arrived back at the reception hall to say our good-byes and were driven by one of Hugh's friends to the Vancouver Hotel where our room was on the 13th floor. Guess we weren't superstitious! Because one of Hugh's friends knew where we were, no sooner had we started to get ready for bed when there was a loud ruckus outside our door and about a dozen of our friends were trying to get into our room through the transom (small window that opened outward above the entrance door to our room). They insisted we let them in or they wouldn't leave, embarrassing me to death, but we won by stubbornly refusing, and they finally went away.

It was so hot in our room we spent half the night hanging out the window to cool off. Not too romantic, to say the least. In the morning we left for Portland by train and discovered, when we got to our hotel, our "double" room we had ordered had twin beds. I was embarrassed again, not only because Hugh had developed laryngitis, but I had to insist we be given another room with a double bed. The only one they found available was a tiny storeroom-like room on the top floor, a far cry from a honeymoon suite!

In the morning we took a bus to Seaside where we spent

a week.   Here again we were surprised with our
accommodations as the bathrooms for all the rooms, in
what proved to be a big old house, were down the hall.
Never ask a bachelor friend for a recommendation!
Hugh's friend, Marcus Robertson had raved about this
North Prom Hotel only a block from the ocean. I will say
the food was delicious and they treated us royally, almost
giving us the key to the city with special coupons for
freebies all over the place.   And since this was the
beginning of May, we were the only guests in the hotel
and we had the beach to ourselves, even if we had to build
forts every day with our beach towels and a blanket to
keep out the cold wind!

Our hostesses were a mother and daughter and the
daughter's boyfriend was generous in taking us up the
coast to Astoria and also back to Portland. This allowed us
to cash in our return bus tickets. Good thing as that was
the only money we had for food while we were overnight
once again in Portland before taking the train back to
Vancouver.

We took a taxi from the train to our little home, paid the
fare and Hugh was left with 50 cents in his pocket.
Needless to say, our first order of business was to take
back some duplicate wedding gifts to have money to live
on until Hugh's paycheck arrived in another week.

Things were going well. We were adjusting to each
other, young and headstrong as we were, and we tried not
to be envious of our friends going off to the beach in the
summer months as we worked liked Trojans on our two
city lots with seven fruit trees, weeding numerous flower
beds and planting a vegetable garden. As the fruit and
vegetables ripened, we made jam and canned the fruit.

We even made tomato juice from our bumper crop of tomatoes and stored away potatoes, like I had seen my parents do, for the coming winter months. By September, however, it was obvious we were not making ends meet and I would have to get a job. I found a secretarial position at the main Police Station.

I had only been there about a month when one morning after getting to work, I felt nauseated, threw up, and had to come home early. You guessed it. I was pregnant. We hadn't planned this, of course, but surprisingly, we were both excited and began to plan for an addition to our family and on August 21, 1952, I delivered a healthy 8 ½ pound baby girl we named Wendy Jean. I had just turned 21 the month before on July 8th.

Around this time Hugh tried reaching out to my father and went on numerous fishing trips with him. On one occasion when they were trolling for trout on a lake, Hugh was getting all the bites on his side of the boat. Finally, in exasperation, Dad said, "Are you saying a prayer to catch those fish?" Hugh just laughed!

Through this friendship, our relationship with my father improved, and when Hugh was promoted and given a raise, we decided our Christmas present to each other would be to put in a bathroom in our closed-in back porch. We approached my dad with trepidation and asked if he'd help us. He said he would.

As I was writing the above paragraph, I was reading Beowulf (A New Telling by Robert Nye of the oldest English epic thought to be composed in the early 8th Century). Unferth, the antagonist, is telling Beowulf that the apple he is eating is from a witch's grove and only "someone wicked could eat witch's apples and come to no harm." But Beowulf, in a calm voice says, "Listen, Unferth...you think that bad brings forth bad only, but...*even the wickedest person can do good for someone*" (italics added).

The Bible confirms this, of course. Genesis 1:17: "God created man in his own image, in the image of God he created him..." Indeed, no one is all bad for they are made in the image of God. And although my dad's actions and words, at times, were mostly "bad," it is true he did good things as well, not only in this instance, but also at other times.

For my first family dinner in our tiny home we moved our kitchen table into the living room where we were able to put two chairs down the sides, without room behind them, and a chair at each end. We had my parents and my sister Mabel and her husband Bill Reid. I tried to get them seated but it was not an easy task as they had to climb over the chairs to their seats. When they decided to change where I had planned for them to sit and I couldn't seem to get them seated, I climbed over the chairs and went into our bedroom with much frustration and cried. I finally calmed myself and came out and tried again, and this time they listened to me and sat down. I was only nineteen, remember?

I can only remember the roasted chicken I served. My dad's comment when he left was, "That's the best shoe leather I ever tasted!" He thought he was being funny. I didn't!

During these early years of our marriage, I called my mother every day. After we had Wendy, she especially delighted in knowing what new milestones she had reached: first tooth, first step, first word, etc. Like mother, like daughter. Wendy, after 27 years of marriage, still likes to call me often and I now know why Mama enjoyed those calls so much!

My mother had many talents besides being the world's best grandmother and cook. She crocheted intricate doilies and large tablecloths and quilted numerous blankets. I still use a couple on our guest beds. And she began what she called her "Nana Series." She would buy a large scrapbook and fill it with pictures she cut out from magazines—everything from a plane to a car, from people of all ages to household items, from furniture to pots and pans, scenes, weather and even a joke or two. The jokes were for the parents to enjoy as we increased our children's vocabulary. They were the greatest. We wore out several with our children. She must have made over a hundred at least as her grandchildren were not the only recipients. She made them for many other toddlers as well. They were truly a labor of love.

After about three years in our tiny home, we realized if we were going to have more children we would have to move. There was no way we could put in another crib or bed in the back bedroom that was about the size of a medium closet.

We put the house up for sale for $3000.00, found another two-bedroom house for $6000.00 on St. Catherines Street and 47th and moved in time to welcome our first son, David Craig, almost 9 lbs., on January 8, 1955. We had been married three and a half years. And that's when we got our first car!

. . . .

Hugh's father felt that now with two children, we needed some transportation and he found a 1936 Ford sedan for $100.00, fixed it up and presented it to us. True, it was old, but to us it was beautiful and even though when it rained I used to joke we needed to have umbrellas because the rain came up under the doors and through the ill-fitting windshield, we loved and appreciated it.

When Wendy was born, Hugh suggested the name Anne. I said, "Not on your life. That's the name of an old girlfriend." He let it drop, but one day after David was born, it suddenly hit me that he had gotten in her name anyway. "Craig" was her last name! Hugh insists he never even thought of that when he suggested Craig as David's middle name. I'm still not at all certain about that!

Wendy was two and a half when David was born and because she had been such a good and easy child to raise, I began to have inflated ideas about my mothering skills! That is, bless him, until David came along. He really threw me for a loop with his independent streak. But it was the best thing that happened to me. It helped me understand that children have different temperaments, and it wasn't necessarily my parenting skills that made Wendy who she was, or David who he was, for that matter!

In those early years, I would read to the children from a little devotional called, "Pete and Penny." One night the emphasis was on giving our hearts to Jesus and since Wendy was a compliant child, always wanting to do what was right, she wanted to pray right then and there to ask Jesus into her heart, which she did. (Later, when she was eight and we were living on Amores Street in Mexico City, she went to a Child Evangelism camp where she reconfirmed her decision to follow Christ.)

Wendy loved to go to Sunday School, so when one Sunday morning our car wouldn't start, she was devastated. We lived in a neighborhood of non-church goers, making it unlikely anyone would be awake to help Hugh jump start the car. It seemed we would just have to stay home.

Wendy, deeply disappointed she couldn't go to Sunday School, began to cry. To calm her, I suggested she pray and ask Jesus to help us get the car started. She wiped her eyes, knelt down by the sofa, folded her hands, shut her eyes and simply said, "Dear Jesus, I want to go to Sunday School. Please fix our car, Amen." She jumped up, turned around and said, "Well, where is He?" Her faith was free of any doubts that Jesus would not do what she asked.

At that point, Hugh came in and said, "Let's go!" He had gone back out to try once more to start the car, and this time it did! That day, through the steadfast faith of our four-year-old daughter, our faith was strengthened and we learned a great lesson in believing, expectant prayer!

During this time I had struggled many sleepless nights wondering if I had kept Hugh from what he really wanted to do. When we were dating, he had told me he felt called to the ministry, but in no way did I feel I was called to be a pastor's wife. Until, that is, one Sunday night when Hugh was home babysitting and I went to the Sunday evening service by myself. Forrest Johnson, a pastor from the Seattle area, was our guest speaker, and he emphasized the importance of yielding our lives completely to the Lord who had given His all for us. I don't remember ever hearing a message like this or grappling with the importance of submission and obedience to God's will.

Coming from a "Closed" Plymouth Brethren background where altar calls were never given, it was foreign to me to even consider walking the aisle, but when Pastor Johnson gave an invitation for those who wanted to follow God's will for their lives publically declare it, I think I was the first one down the aisle. What a relief I felt! I had finally said, "Yes," to God to fit in with His plan for me and I knew Hugh would be so happy.

How wrong I was! I got home and told him what I did and his response was, "You did what?"

"I went down front and made a public decision to follow God wherever He might lead us," I said with a big smile. "I know you've been thinking about the pastorate, but his emphasis was on missions, so I thought maybe that's what we could do."

"Well, you're mistaken," said Hugh. "I no longer feel called to be a pastor and being a missionary is that last thing I want to be!"

What followed was a very difficult fifth year of marriage. I kept nagging him and we'd both become angry at each other.

Finally, one day, as I was praying, it was as if the Lord said to me, "If you quit talking so much, maybe he'll hear Me." I did, and before long, we both began to read missionary biographies and Hugh began to earnestly pray about the possibility of cross-cultural mission service.

About a year later, Ruth Morton Baptist Church called a new pastor, Rev. William Sloan, who held our church's first mission conference. We heard many speakers explain about their missions and work, and amazingly, we were both separately impressed with the work of Wycliffe Bible Translators. Ralph and Vera Borthwick were Ruth Morton members and had gone out with Wycliffe to Peru five years earlier with two small children. Ralph, a pilot, transported missionaries and supplies to and from villages while Vera worked in the offices. They talked and showed slides about "support workers" who worked on Wycliffe centers around the world as accountants, printers, buyers, pilots, mechanics or radio operators. Some joined Wycliffe to help out with maintenance; others were teachers, doctors, and much more. This allowed the translators to stay out in the villages as Bible translators. We talked it over when we got home and felt perhaps there would be somewhere where we could fit in and contribute to the overall work of Bible translation.

Interestingly, Hugh at this time was beginning to get interested in radio broadcasting and had a couple of good auditions, so when Ralph Borthwick mentioned Wycliffe's need of a radio operator in Peru, we thought perhaps this would be where God would lead us. I could help out with my secretarial skills.

We prayed about it, came to a meeting of the minds, and questioned the Borthwicks where we should begin the process of getting connected with Wycliffe. This was now June 1956. Vera suggested we write Mr. Townsend.

Two and a half weeks later, in a letter dated June 17, 1956, we received a letter from Mrs. Townsend:

Dear Mr. & Mrs. Steven:
I have your good letter of June 10th before me and we certainly are rejoicing over the way the Lord is leading

. . . .

you. It is certainly true that we need a radio operator at the Base and stenographers are always in demand.

You asked what the next step should be. I would suggest that you write to Mr. Howard Law, Canadian Camp Wycliffe [now the Summer Institute of Linguistics], Caronport, Saskatchewan, Canada and see if there is any chance of you still being able to take our linguistic course this summer at Caronport. Classes start on Monday but it might still be possible for you to attend. After taking the course, the Board decides whether your qualifications are acceptable. It might be that they would suggest at that time that you have some Bible training. That would possibly depend on your Bible exam. But don't let that scare you. If Mr. Law feels that it is too late for you to take the course this year, he will no doubt suggest how you can use the coming year most profitably and then take the course next year. All of our workers, whether doing language work or not, must take the linguistic course.

I trust I shall have the pleasure of meeting you some day and working together in His vineyard.

> In His joy,
> (Signed) Mrs. W.C. Townsend

A funny P.S. to this story is that years later we showed Elaine Townsend this letter. She laughed and said, "I can't believe I told you to do this. I really didn't have the authority."

We did write Howard Law and he told us to come to Caronport right away. Hugh wasn't sure we would be able to as he would have to give a two-week notice at

Woodward's, but off he went to work to tell them what we were about to do. And Hugh has his first testing.

"I hope you know what you're doing," said his boss. "A raise came through for you today."

As it turned out, when his boss heard the whole story, he told Hugh he could leave that very day and for him to come back when we had finished our two-month linguistic course. Hugh did, and they took him back at the raise he would have been given if he hadn't left!

But now there were still bills to pay, and we needed someone to rent the house. Fortunately, right at that time Hugh's brother Jim, newly married, was looking for accommodation, and he agreed to move in and look after our home.

The weekend we were finally ready to leave was July 1st, a national holiday in Canada. Hugh naively went to the train station to buy our tickets and the man told him that he was sorry but with it being a holiday weekend, there was absolutely no room or berths available. "But just a minute," he said. "Let me check to see if we have a cancellation."

And sure enough there was one and we were set, at least to buy one-way tickets for the four of us after paying off our bills and having enough to pay for our lodging and linguistics course at Briercrest Bible Institute where the Summer Institute of Linguistics (SIL), Wycliffe's sister organization, held its course in Canada.

Wendy was 4, David 1 ½ and Hugh and I were 25. In the space of two and a half weeks our whole lives were turned upside down.

There were many tears as we said good-bye to our families and friends but what an encouragement when about 50 friends from Ruth Morton Baptist Church came to see us off. We were green behind the ears about train travel so it was comforting to have Ralph Borthwick show us where to put our baggage (most of which was cardboard boxes with ropes tied around them) and get us settled on the train. And then, with his limited missionary finances, he pressed $10.00 into Hugh's hand--a sacrifice for him, a blessing for us to be able to get a meal on the train.

Added to Hugh's boss letting him quit the very day he put in his notice, Hugh's brother agreeing to look after the house on such short notice, and the unexpected cancellation on a holiday weekend enabling us to get to Caronport, were Scripture verses that gave us a settled conviction we were going in the right direction. The following two were especially meaningful:

> Ask of me, and I shall give thee the heathen for thine inheritance, and the uttermost parts of the earth for thy possession (Psalm 2:8, KJV).

> You will go out in joy and be led forth in peace; the mountains and hills will burst into song before you, and all the trees of the field will clap their hands (Isaiah 55:12, KJV).

As the train sped through the Rockies and on out into the prairies that July 1, 1956 night, my mind was filled with these verses, and the next morning as we were nearing our destination, I looked out on the fields of wheat as far as the eye could see and said to Hugh, "Look! No trees are clapping, but how about that wheat?" It was gently swaying in the wind and indeed looked as if the stalks were clapping their hands.

We had stepped out into the unknown with some fear, yet also with joy and peace as we knew we were being obedient to what God was giving us to do.

8

Linguistics, Cucumbers, Mexico

We stepped off the train onto a wooden platform in Caron, Saskatchewan, three miles northwest of Caronport, our destination. Our "luggage" was strewn by the side of the tracks many cars ahead where it had been thrown off the baggage car. And there the four of us stood--wind howling and nothing else as far as the eyes could see but prairie and one lone silo.

In 2009, Caron had a population of 120. No telling how many lived there in 1956. As far as we could see, it looked like the population was zero. There was no evidence of telephone poles and certainly no cell phones, Iphones, Blackberrys or other devices to remind the folks in Caronport we had arrived. I felt forgotten, forlorn and foolish as I stood in my high heels and a new coat and dress to match I had made, wearing a hat and gloves. It was hardly suitable for our new adventure that looked like it may never get off the ground.

Finally, with tired, hungry, whimpering children and Hugh and I looking helplessly at each other, our spirits soared as we heard the approach of a vehicle. Was it our ride to the Summer Institute of Linguistics? In anticipation we stood at the ready. I'm sure our faces reflected our disappointment when our rescuer turned out to be an old farmer in a beat-up station wagon. However, he was more than happy to take our cartons and suitcases to Briercrest Bible Institute in Caronport where we were scheduled to begin Wycliffe's 10-week linguistic course (now only eight weeks for us) for new recruits.

We were in for two shocks when we arrived on campus. One was the forlorn look on students' faces. The other was having our luggage fumigated. While Hugh tried to discover why everyone seemed to be discouraged, I tried to hold back my tears that our luggage was being sprayed. Did they really think we were carrying fleas or lice? What kind of people did they think we were? Finally someone told us it was the school's policy and they had all experienced the fumigation two weeks earlier when they arrived.

As for the abject students, their response to Hugh's questioning was, "Just wait until Monday when you start your studies. You'll understand."

And quickly we did! Added to our trauma of beginning our studies with students who were two weeks ahead of us, for two weeks in the evenings we had to catch up on the material we had missed. And we had the pain of leaving Wendy and David in the nursery where they were most unhappy (I could hear David crying a block away in our classroom). I began to wonder if we had made a mistake in understanding God's will for our lives.

Somehow we survived. I did very well on the linguistics, not so well on the Bible exam. Hugh did very well on the Bible exam and anthropology courses, not so well on the linguistics. Nevertheless we filled out our application to Wycliffe at the end of the summer and left it in God's hands. And then we had our interview with Otis Leal, the then Secretary for Recruitment.

He chatted a while and asked us about how we enjoyed our summer. His next statement shocked us. "I've looked over your application forms and I don't feel we have a place for you in Wycliffe."

After all we'd been through, believing we were exactly where God had led us, we couldn't believe it. I can't remember what we said. I think I was in shock. All I remember is walking back to our room, throwing myself on our bed and weeping. "How can he say that we've made a mistake," I wailed. "I know God led us into Wycliffe and has a place for us." Hugh remained quiet. He recalls feeling hollow inside, sick, bewildered, not knowing what to make of it.

I don't think we slept much that night. Early the next morning there was a knock on the door. I opened it and there stood Otis. I wasn't too happy to see him, but he asked to come in.

"I don't know what to say," Otis began. "I confess at your interview I hadn't read all the information on your work experience and after going through your application again, I realize I've made a big mistake. We do feel there's a place for you. Not in Peru, but in Mexico where we need a buyer and the director needs a secretary."[5]

Needless to say, we were relieved, and peace once again returned that we were on the right track. In hindsight I do believe this was God giving us an opportunity to solidify our decision that He was really calling us into mission service with Wycliffe.

During our weeks at SIL, we had received a few monetary gifts from friends who knew of our need, so it was no surprise in our journey of faith when enough money came in to pay for our return tickets. There was nothing left over, however, for food on the train, so when the camp kitchen personnel said they had just baked some fresh bread and we could make sandwiches, off went Hugh to do just that while I continued to pack.

A few days earlier I had commented to Hugh that I loved cucumbers in sandwiches, and he remembered. He put cucumbers with every combination he made, except for the peanut butter and jelly sandwiches for the children. We were well set, especially when Katie Keller, our phonetics teacher, gave us an extra $2.00 to buy ice cream on the train for the children.

Hugh made the sandwiches the night before, and after going into Moose Jaw, 26 kilometers east of Caron to catch the late afternoon train, we were on our way home to Vancouver. We had a good night's sleep on the train with me waking up Hugh in the middle of the night to watch the Northern Lights, and in the morning we pulled out our sandwiches that would be our breakfast. At least we thought they were going to be! We were disappointed

---

[5] Years later, Otis told us that because of Hugh's many publications, we were, in his words, "a national treasure."

however, to discover that cucumber on fresh bread is not a good combination! The sandwiches were completely soggy and inedible. The children had their peanut butter and jelly sandwiches, and we used the $2.00 from Katie to buy a sandwich for ourselves. We arrived around noon the next day. I can't remember when we finally got to eat something, but I'm sure we were famished!

Next came the selling of our house. We priced it at $8000.00 and prayed for a buyer. Around October, Wendy came down with measles and we still hadn't had any interested customers. We knew David would be coming down with measles in a couple of weeks and hoped perhaps in between Wendy getting better and David coming down with them, a buyer would appear. And God sent one, just another one of His many blessings we experienced along the way.

We met with our church's mission committee to discuss that Wycliffe is a "faith" mission and each person is responsible to raise their own support. At a church meeting it was decided they would support us $200.00 a month. Since this was our only church contact, we wondered how we would manage on $200.00 a month for the four of us, but we praised God for this provision and would trust Him for the rest. A year later when we came home to wait for our Mexico permanent papers, we would be lowered to $100.00, as were all the missionaries they supported, and the church board wondered whether or not we really needed our car. We were taken aback by that remark, but Hugh assured them it was our transportation down and also while in Mexico City for him to transport the supplies he bought for missionaries.

It was surprising to me as well, and actually difficult to realize, people were watching to see if we were spending "their" money correctly. At times I felt like a charity case. I remember one trip home when we were still wearing hats to church, someone came up to me and said, "Wow! How can you afford that hat, being a missionary?" It was a lovely velour hat I borrowed from my sister Eileen and I hated having to defend myself. Most, of course, never made us feel that way, but I remember sharing my feelings once with our friend Phyllis Gettig.

"I do wish we were on a salary," I said. "I don't like having to depend on donors for our livelihood."

"Oh, Norma," she said, "don't feel that way. We've got to have someone to give to!" Somehow her statement was comforting and I've never forgotten it. I knew what a joy it was for us to give to others. And I began to understand we weren't depending on others, as much as having the privilege of learning to depend upon God.

One thing I learned about breaking up our home is that we put so much stock in our possessions, but when it comes right down to it, they aren't worth all that much. We were surprised at how little cash we realized from the sale of our used furniture. We had bought a new washing machine and stove just before going off to Caronport to study linguistics, and these Hugh's brother took. My parents took our kitchen chrome table set that Hugh's parents had given us our first Christmas, and also the drapes that my friend Audrey Renney had made. We stored some of our nicer things and mementos with friends John and Thelma Scott and in Hugh's mother's basement (which later her new husband, whom she married after Hugh's father's death, threw out), and set January 1, 1957,

New Year's Day, as our date for leaving to head down south to Mexico. We then moved in with my parents until we left.

I was into knitting heavy "Indian" sweaters at that time and knitted one for David and my dad that Christmas before we left. I was still struggling with my inability to forgive him, but I thought perhaps knitting this sweater would be a practical way of reaching out to him with Christ's love and make me feel less hostile to him.

It was a cold, wet New Year's Day in 1957 when we said goodbye. David was bundled up in his sweater and matching toque. Both he and Wendy had a nice place in the back seat of the panel delivery truck Hugh's father had helped us buy.

By the time we reached Bakersfield in California, David shed his sweater and toque and I don't think he ever wore them again! Another thing I remember about leaving our families is crying practically all the way down to Seattle. It was hard, even though we knew this was where God was leading us.

We stopped in Modesto, California to see our friends, Ramona and Mel Turner, whom we had met at SIL in Caronport. They would be going to the Philippines where Mel would be a pilot, but they were still raising their support.

Two things I remember from that visit. It was our first experience with how Americans, at least the Turners, made tea. We were taught to rinse the teapot with hot water before putting in either loose tea or tea bags, then to fill the teapot with boiling water and let it steep for five minutes. We sat down to "tea" to a cup filled with hot water and the tea was passed around in a little silver ball with each person dunking it into their cup of hot water a few times.   That took some getting used to for us Canadians!

The other experience we have never forgotten was how David, who celebrated his second birthday on the way down to Mexico, swallowed a whole bottle of baby aspirin. The bedroom we were in at the Turners was quite small and they had a crib that was pushed up to a dresser. David, hyperactive and into everything at that age, reached over and got the bottle sitting on the dresser and we came in to find the bottle empty.   Hugh and Mel rushed him to a doctor's office where his stomach was pumped.   Hugh remembers how strong David was and how difficult it was for him to hold him down.   And can you believe, David almost got another bottle of baby aspirin a second time! My fault for leaving it where he could climb up and get it.

Our first crossing of the Mexican border was a nightmare, as were all the others, for the most part, and I have to say that after many crossings, when we left Mexico in 1968, I was not unhappy to leave that behind. We had sold the old 1936 Ford Sedan to Hugh's friend Phil Chiddell for $75.00 and we had another friend, Mr. Stangeland, build us a roof rack that completely covered the roof of our panel delivery truck.   We piled on everything we felt we would be needing to set up housekeeping, plus clothes, books and toys for the children, and Hugh covered it all with a large tarp, tying it securely.

Since we didn't have our permanent papers yet, we went in on tourist visas and this caused somewhat of a problem for the Mexican border officials who couldn't understand, if we were tourists, why we were taking dishes, pots and pans and other household goods. They made Hugh take everything down and there we were, all our worldly goods spread around us, waiting for the officials to give us the okay to continue with our trip. But they weren't about to give us permission without a tip, and with our limited Spanish and inexperience crossing borders, it took some time before they got their message across. Hugh can't remember how much he paid them, but he thinks about ten pesos each, and we were on our way. It took us seven days of driving from Vancouver to reach our desitination—Mexico City.

I still remember coming into Mexico City. Traffic seemed to have no rhyme or reason and was coming at us from every direction. At one point I was so nervous, I put my head down in my lap. Finally we arrived at the door of Wycliffe's Mexico City Headquarters, an old converted hotel they called "The Kettle." There was no room in the "inn" so we spent the first week in a hotel around the corner until a small two-room apartment opened up in the headquarters, and we set up housekeeping.

We had a double bed and two bunks in the bedroom, a small living room and a bathroom with a shelf that came down over the tub where we would cook breakfast and lunch on our camp stove. We ate dinner in the common dining room. The single girls' dorm was on the floor above us and years later they told us they could hear everything going on in our bedroom as there was a drain pipe that went right down the wall past our bed. I didn't need to know that!

Group living was an adjustment, but we knew we were where we should be, and God enabled us to adjust, begin to learn Spanish and get involved in the work. Hugh was immediately inducted into the Buyer's office buying supplies for the missionaries out in the villages translating the Scriptures. He was asked at times to provide everything from birthday presents to a prosthesis, a water pump or other equipment, but most often it was medicines and food supplies. As he built up the work and we moved to new headquarters, Hugh became what he called a "pharmacist without portfolio" as he set up a room with sample medicines he had procured from pharmaceutical companies and doctors for missionaries who used them in their village clinics. One company even gave him the sterling recipe for making worm medicine. He would make it up in a big barrel, one hundred liters at a time, and saved the missionaries hundreds of dollars. In our new headquarters, he also ran a small commissary for household staples.

While Hugh was out looking for bargains and combing Mexico City streets to fill the orders that came in, I was busy with Wendy and David and also assigned as the director's secretary. Sometimes I would work into the night to get the letters done as there was no time during the day. I also worked in the Publications Department where I did paste-up work and designed covers for primers. And I spent many hours typing up masters for printing the translated Scripture portions.

It took me three months to type the Gospel of John in the Trique language. We only had paper masters in those days and I typed (manually) the text leaving spaces for the five tones (indicated with numbers 1-5), then I'd put in the masters again and type in the numbers, and lastly I used

. . . .

another typewriter with a smaller type to put in the Spanish at the bottom of this diglot version. How much easier with the advent of computers!

I also learned the Dewey Decimal System and became the group librarian at our new headquarters for a couple of years. Lastly, I was Hugh's secretary as his work expanded.

It didn't take us long to feel we were immersed in the work and a vital part of Wycliffe's translation ministry in Mexico. Three months after we arrived, we were asked to go out to the Indian village of San Gregorio where Katie Voigtlander and Vola Griste were translating the Scriptures for a group of Otomi Indians. There was a need for chickens to be inoculated against cholera and Hugh did the job. "Easier on chickens than people," was Hugh's response to the assigned task.

It was a lengthy, harrowing trip giving me an insight into how some missionaries had to go in and out of their villages where there weren't airstrips. First we went on the curviest road we'd ever been on for about six hours. Wendy kept saying, "Don't go around the curve! Just go through the mountain!" She really was "green around the gills" and we had to stop several times to let her throw up.

We stayed overnight in the little town of Huehuetla where there was only one hotel. Unusual for me, I had a migraine headache. I figured it was from going around so many curves. All I wanted to do was crawl into bed. When I did, the sheets were damp and it was then I noticed the mold on the walls. I decided to lay on top of the covers!

The only bathroom was down the hall, but that didn't bother Wendy. She found two chamber pots in cupboards on either side of the hotel room and exulted, "Look, there's one for mommy and daddy and one for David and me!"

The next morning, after a sleepless night, we boarded our rickety plane. Through the floor boards we could see the tree tops and only later learned that some pilots flew drunk as the planes were not serviced as they should be and many had lost their lives. Then it was a four-hour trek on horses. We went in and out of a river for two hours and another two hours straight up a mountain.

I had Wendy sitting in front of me; Hugh took David in front of him. By the time I alit from the horse, I could hardly walk as my backside was raw from rubbing on the wooden saddle. This was the first time I had ever been on a horse. I wondered why Hugh was always wanting me to ride horses with him!

Wendy was quite the novelty while we were in the village. Most of the people there had not seen a blue-eyed child before. She made fast friends with a little Indian girl her age by the name of Malia though not a word was spoken between them. I was so fascinated with the Otomi embroidered blouses and skirts, Vola Grist, the Wycliffe missionary, made me an outfit the couple of days we were there.

On the way home, the Indians were using dynamite

to fish. My horse was so spooked, he took off with Wendy and me up the mountainside before I could get him stopped. I don't know if I was saying "whoa" or something else!

As the weeks went by I felt Wendy should be in preschool learning Spanish. When someone told us about a good French kindergarten close by, I enrolled her. I should not have been surprised when a few days later she came home and announced she had learned a new word. Excited that she was already learning Spanish, I asked her what it was.

"Gr-r-randmother-r-r," she said, trilling her "r's." We laughed and laughed. We thought she'd learn Spanish but she was learning English! Because we had paid for a month, we kept her there, but she was glad when she didn't have to go any more. Her blue eyes and long blond hair were a novelty for the Mexican children. "They always want to stroke my hair and look at my eyes," she'd complain.

One night as I was tucking her into bed, she said, "I wish there were steps going up and down to heaven. Then when kids are mean and I'm sad, I could go and sit on Jesus' lap." I think we've all felt that way at one time or another!

In July 1957, my mother came for a three-week visit. She met a lot of people and made good friends with several with whom she wrote to for years. We did a lot of touristy things like see the pyramids, the university, and shop in the colorful markets. It was a wonderful experience for her and best of all her doubts about whether or not I'd make a missionary were put to rest. "I often wondered if

Norma had what it took to be a missionary," she commented before leaving, "but when I saw how she had to cook in the bathroom with the children running in and out, and live in this tiny place, I knew she was going to be okay."

In February 1958, we finally got around to taking our mandatory Jungle Camp training. For six weeks we lived in a thatched-roof mud hut at "Main Base" while we learned carpentry, mechanics, swimming, canoeing, Spanish, jungle cooking, saddling, and how to ride mules (I could have used the latter a year earlier when we went on our first village visit!). We had a medical course where we learned about everything from how to treat burns, fractures, tropical diseases and how to give injections, practicing on each other. But our training was much more than just practical skills we might need. It was also cross-cultural training designed to help us learn how to adapt to the culture in which we lived and worked.

That's Norma in the middle (patterned skirt) of the photo bending over with a knife skinning the cow's leg!

The hardest tasks for me were learning to kill a chicken with a machete, then pluck, clean and cut it up, and butchering a cow. I tried three times to help butcher a cow and each time I would get so nauseated I had to go and lie down. Then one day one of the staff gave a talk using Philippians 4:13, "I can do all things through Christ who gives me strength," and armed with this verse, the next time I was on the crew that skinned the cow, I repeated that verse at least twenty times until I got through my task. The worst part was examining myself afterwards and getting rid of the ticks that had crawled onto me from the cow.

After six weeks at Main Base it was on to our "Advance Base" where we built our own hut ("champa" as it was called) and furniture out of poles and bamboo canes, and for six more weeks we put into practice what we had learned at Main Base. Quite an experience with two small children!

A special memory I have is of spending Easter at Advance Base. Hugh got up early Easter morning and walked two hours to a village to buy a chicken and six eggs (it was against the camp rules but after our course we discovered they had us down as only two people, when we were four, and when they doled out the food, we did not get enough and were always running out. Hugh actually lost seven pounds in six weeks!).

We had been studying Spanish at a language school and a private tutor, but there was another language we had to learn if we wanted to stay in the country. SIL's contract said that each member would learn one of the ethnic languages. We were assigned to a parched valley in

Wendy, David and Norma with the "spoils" of Hugh's 2-hour trek
to get a few goodies for Easter. Wendy is holding her basket,
Norma has the chicken, and the bouquet of flowers is on the stump
On the way back, Hugh picked me a bouquet of wild flowers and we
had a wonderful celebration. We hard- boiled the eggs, and the
children colored them with their Crayolas. I made a basket for each of
them by cutting a round oatmeal box in half.

Central Mexico where 90,000 Otomi Indians lived, about
100 miles northeast of Mexico City. In 1959, there were
about one thousand believers in this area so we attended
several churches and meeting places, visited the believers
in their homes and even helped pick tomatoes, all the
while learning Otomi. We spent four summers out there,
leaving Wendy with some new friends, Ed and Margaret
Pentecost, in Mexico City. They were with Inter-Varsity
and later Ed went into plastics. Their daughter Lois
became Wendy's good friend and we thought this would
be an ideal situation for her. But Wendy will tell you to
this day she still has difficulty being separated from
extended family. It was a hard thing for her, but
fortunately it was only for two months each year. She did
get to come out a couple of times during those two months

and with David enjoyed the dogs, pigs, chickens, burros and goats.

Over the years we had several friends visit us in Mexico. We remember how Jay and Verna Perkins from Vancouver, B.C. came to visit us for a week in 1959. Verna had been Hugh's Sunday School teacher at Ruth Morton Baptist Church when he first made a commitment to Christ, so she always had a special place in Hugh's heart. And they were some of our first individual donors. We took them out to visit with two Otomi Christian families. One of the older Christian men told us, through the Wycliffe missionary Nancy Lanier interpreting for him, how he was once drunk all the time, but since he had taken Jesus into his heart, he didn't do that anymore and he was sure that soon he would be seeing His Savior. Surely his life was a display of God's splendor!

In 1959 we were able to find a small apartment outside the Kettle. We felt we needed more room and found an apartment with delightful landlords, Homer and Jane Argudin. Here we added a new member to our family on April 12, 1962--Lee Anthony Steven, weight 6 lbs., 12 oz., whom we quickly dubbed, "Little Lee." We had decided since we had Wendy and David when we were just 21 and 22, and before we knew it they would be going stateside to school, we should add another member to our family. Trouble was there was absolutely no place to put a crib in our little rented apartment. He remained in a bassinette on top of a chest of drawers until Wycliffe's new headquarters were built and we were able to move into one of the two-bedroom apartments just in time for Lee to graduate to a larger crib. Later we put a standing partition in Wendy and David's bedroom and David and Lee had bunks while

Wendy had her privacy on the other side.

There were two memorable incidents that took place while living in this little apartment on Amores Street (Street of Loves) that stood next door to a "motel" on the other side of a high brick fence. We soon found out it was actually a brothel, but we tried not to think about that. The high fence helped!

The first is that David at age four did not want to go to heaven unless he could take his new tricycle and four goldfish he received for his birthday. But by five, one morning, while I walked him to his kindergarten, he said, "I want to ask Jesus into my heart." Delighted, I said, "We can do that right now." "No! No!" he said. "I want to do it when we get home from school."

David, ever independent, would want to do everything by himself and let me know in no uncertain terms, "I can do it self me!" He would have told me sooner if he could have talked, but he didn't until about the age of three. He wanted to do everything on his own timetable. And true to his word, he came home from Kindergarten, got down by his bunk bed and prayed a simplified version of the sinner's prayer, repeating it after me. He then got up and with a happy smile on his face went out to play and has been a follower of Jesus ever since!

The other incident was of a different genre. One morning Hugh woke up ill with extreme abdominal pain and was unable to go to work. I wanted to call the doctor (who still made house calls), but our finances were so minimal, Hugh felt I should wait. After our Jungle Camp training, when we had gone back to Vancouver in 1958 to get our resident papers for Mexico, our church, Ruth Morton Baptist, lowered our monthly support, and all other missionaries they supported, to $100.00 per month. A couple of the church members, unhappy with this, promised to send their gifts directly to us through Wycliffe. We were grateful that by the time we were back in Mexico, our support was almost back up to the $200.00 a month we had been promised in 1957 when we left for Mexico. Nevertheless, even with unexpected gifts coming through for us at times, we were not making ends meet. We continued to go "into the red" some months (fortunately Wycliffe allowed us to do this at that time).

By the afternoon, Hugh was crawling to get to the bathroom to throw up and I called the doctor over his protests. It only took a few moments for the doctor to make a diagnosis. Acute Appendicitis. He immediately drove Hugh in his own car to the hospital, where he performed an appendectomy on Hugh's almost ruptured appendix.

Meanwhile, back home, I got Wendy and David settled at the home of a Mexican neighbor we barely knew. I would have left them with our landlords, the Argudins, but they were not home. I hailed a taxi and got to the American British Cowdray (ABC) Hospital where Hugh was already in the ward recuperating.

We discussed, and fretted, about how we would pay the doctor and hospital bills, prayed, and I left to hail a cab to get me back home. It was about 7:00 p.m., already dark, and men were getting off work. Try as I might, I could not get a cab. Every time I thought I had one, someone would jump in ahead of me. After about an hour of this, I was begging God to help me get home. I began to worry about leaving the children such a long time, especially since I wasn't too sure about the people with whom I had left

· ·

them. I only knew them through their own children who had played with Wendy and David a couple of times.

I was fighting back tears by the time I finally settled into a cab and arrived back home. Wendy and David were crying when I picked them up at 8:30. They hadn't eaten and thought I wasn't coming back.

I fed them and got them into bed and then knelt down by my bed and the dam broke. I sobbed in anger feeling abandoned by God. "You know we don't have money to pay the doctor or hospital," I said through my tears. "And why didn't you help me get a cab? The children were so upset. You don't care! You just don't care!"

I crawled into bed and cried myself to sleep, still angry at God, knowing I shouldn't let "the sun go down on my wrath," but I was too upset to care.

I awoke the next morning feeling terribly guilty about my hostile attitude toward God. I knew it wasn't right and got down on my knees and confessed my sin. "Please forgive me," I prayed. "I don't want to be mad at You. I know You love me and I'm going to trust You." A great wave of peace washed over me and I knew somehow we were going to get through this crisis.

The next day when I went back to the hospital, I was able to leave the children with our landlords. When I arrived, Hugh told me the pastor of Union Church, Rev. Frank Wood, had been in to see him and had casually asked how we were doing financially.

"He was shocked our support was so low," said Hugh, "and he felt sure Union Church could help us in some way."

This was wonderful news, and when Hugh told me someone from Union Church had also paid the doctor bill,

I knew I had been mistaken the night before. God *did* care! And later Union Church (where we were associate members and taught Sunday School), did find a way to help us. They took on our support for $200.00 a month!

About this time, some good Wycliffe friends, Ray and Kay Larson, invited us to come up to their area in northern Mexico to visit them. While there, someone gave us a cute Pekingese puppy we promptly named "Juguete," (who-**get**-tay) "toy" in Spanish. He quickly became Wendy's dog. He would let Wendy dress him up in doll clothes, including a bonnet, and play "school" with him. She'd say "stay" and Juguete obeyed until "school" was over, and he'd come when called. It was our first dog and I quickly learned how much a member of the family a dog becomes. My favorite thing to do with him was get him to sing/howl. I'd begin to sing and he'd join in and we'd all end in gales of laughter.

By the summer of 1963, we felt the need for a short furlough since both of us were feeling stressed and worn out. We thought going home for the summer to see our parents, friends, donors and family after a five-year absence was just what we needed. It was, but the trip north was more difficult than expected. Unknown to us, Hugh, Wendy and I were all coming down with infectious hepatitis, and how Hugh was able to drive the seven days from Mexico City to Vancouver, B.C., Canada, was purely by God's grace.

. . . .

9

Hepatitis, Family Addition, Friends, Convent

We stopped by Hugh's parents' home in Vancouver on our way to my parents' home in Maple Ridge. Hugh immediately went downstairs to lie down, I fainted, and Wendy sat languishing on the sofa. What an entrance we made! We didn't know what was wrong with us. We thought it was perhaps the flu and we would recuperate in a day or two. But we didn't. I was weak and then I jaundiced and knew I needed to see a doctor. It was from Mama's doctor we learned we had infectious hepatitis and he told me I needed to go on complete bed rest immediately. Wendy seemed to have a light case and Hugh, though weak, was able to carry on and care for Lee who was just over a year old. I remembered seeing a couple in Mexico who had hepatitis and couldn't get out of bed, yet they didn't look that sick. Now I was experiencing the very same thing. I told someone it felt like three cases of the worst flu you ever had—all at once—and there was a dull pain in my liver.

My father was away on a fishing trip at the time and would be coming home in a week. Knowing his disposition, my mother was concerned about his reaction to finding us in the house with an infectious disease. She thought it best that we leave to keep the peace.

We weren't sure where we could go or who would want us, but once more we called on our friends, John and Thelma Scott as we knew Thelma's mother had a one-bedroom suite in their basement and was away on a vacation in England. We asked if we could move in until we found something else and they graciously obliged even though it meant that they and about 10 or 11 others had to get gamma globulin shots for having been exposed to us. Not a way to win friends and influence people! Wendy, during the next couple of weeks, got over her illness, and Hugh, while still not 100%, carried on looking after the family.

Later, when Thelma's mother returned, we moved into a motel on Kingsway in Burnaby that had two tiny bedrooms and a living-kitchen large room. It was $35.00 a week and many times we marveled we had the money to pay the rent.

Hugh had a crash course in cooking. He did very well except for one day when he tried to remember how his Grandma Steven made Scotch Broth. He put a whole bag of barley in a pot and covered it with water. It was like the "Magic Porridge Pot." It just kept expanding and expanding. As it did, he got out another pot and another until he had so much he could have fed all the people in the motel complex! Only he and Lee liked it, so after they had their fill for several days, the rest was tossed.

The blessing of being in a motel was that we had a cleaning lady. We looked for further help from our church in Vancouver, but it seemed most were too afraid to come around in case they caught what we had. We couldn't

· ·

blame them. However, my dear friend and former work-mate, Irene Brummitt, told her Presbyterian church ladies our plight and they kept our shelves stocked with groceries and baking for the months we were there. And how grateful I was that Irene came over once a week to iron (not as many perma-press clothes in those days!).

We spent Christmas 1963 in the motel. We didn't think we'd have much of a Christmas, but when my sister Eileen showed up with a small tree already trimmed and an armload of gifts, I knew it was going to be okay.

There were several special blessings during these months. One was that Lee was such a good boy, I thought perhaps he must be an angel and God would take him once I got well. He'd sit by the hour with a box of toys, taking one out at a time and putting them back in before getting another. And we couldn't be downhearted when he awoke each morning with a smile and a "hi."

Another blessing was that we had extra time with Hugh's father who, at age 60, would pass away unexpectedly after three heart attacks, one after the other, six months after our return to Mexico.

I learned many good things during our Jungle Camp training, but one thing particularly helped me during the five months flat on my back. I was reminded that I can indeed do all things through Christ who gives me strength.

After five months on complete bed rest and another two months trying to get my strength back, we left in April 1964 to travel back to Mexico. Our two-month furlough had turned into seven months. In May 1964, in a newsletter to our friends and donors, I wrote:

> Our health improves daily. Hugh is able to carry on a full day's work and I feel the old energy

returning. The children are happy to be back with their friends and settled into their old school once more. Lee celebrated his second birthday two weeks ago and proudly holds up two fingers and says "two" when asked how old he is!

One of the things we did over the years to remind people to pray for us was to make a prayer card with our photo and Wycliffe's Canadian and Mexico addresses. Just before leaving for Mexico, we had the one below made.

HUGH AND NORMA STEVEN, LEE, DAVID AND WENDY

By the summer of 1964 we had moved, along with Juguete, into Wycliffe's new Mexico Branch Headquarters. Hugh's new medicine room was bulging with all the sample medicines he had collected from doctor's offices that missionaries could take free of charge for their medical work out in the villages. And his station wagon, given to us by First Baptist in Yucaipa, California, two years previously, was loaded daily with many packages to be mailed to the translators out in the villages.

Hugh, with two helpers, loads supplies he's bought for missionaries into our station wagon. Photo taken when Wycliffe moved their headquarters out to Tlalpan on the outskirts of Mexico City.

We settled into our new furnished apartment but I think the family was ready to turn me in because shortly after we moved in I was in bed another month with paratyphoid. Then I had a tonsillectomy, along with colitis and a bunch of other intestinal "bugs." I wrote in a newsletter that I really hadn't had a chance to get on my feet since being ill with hepatitis.

The tonsillectomy was unforgettable. In preparation, the doctor instructed Hugh to give me a daily shot for a week in order to thicken my blood to make sure it would coagulate. Hugh later commented it's a wonder it didn't give me a stroke with my blood being so thick!

The tonsillectomy would be done in the doctor's office and I was told to bring a towel and a box of Kleenex. When Hugh and I arrived, the waiting room was full, but I was called in, given a shot and told to go out to the waiting room to await my turn. I remember getting sleepier and sleepier and when I couldn't keep my eyes open any longer, I snuggled into the overstuffed chair and fell asleep.

I don't know how long it was before they awakened me and took me into the operating room where they sat me on a straight-back white metal chair, still in my street clothes. They pinned my towel around my neck and told me to hold the Kleenex box in my lap. When the doctor pulled out a very long needle with which to "freeze" the tonsil area, I opened my mouth, shut my eyes and waited for him to finish the operation. And then I heard him tell the nurse to call in Hugh.

Always interested in medicine and medical procedures, Hugh stood behind the doctor and peered over the doctor's shoulder as he cleaned up the back of my throat, and that's when I noticed the blood draining out of Hugh's face. I knew what was coming next. Hugh was about to faint and I guess my wide eyes alerted the doctor to look behind him.

The next thing I knew, I was left swaying in the chair, trying to keep erect, while Hugh was taken out to lie down. Eventually the doctor came back, finished the job and I was escorted out to an uncomfortable couch where they handed me a plastic dish in case I got sick. I'm not sure how long I was left to recuperate. I just know I felt

. . . .

miserable, and in the next couple of days I thought having a tonsillectomy was worse than having a baby. The pain was excruciating.

On October 24, 1964, Hugh's father, Dave, passed away. Sadly, Hugh was four hours too late getting to Vancouver to say "good-bye." In Mexico I lay on our bed and wept when I heard the news. He was such a kind man. I felt closer to him than my own father. One of the missionaries, who lived in the apartment below us, heard me weeping and came up to see what was going on. When I told her, she said, "You just need to put it to the joy account!" I remember thinking, *Well, that didn't help!*

As I thought about it later I realized what a gift tears are. They're a catharsis. A way to heal. This same woman ended her life mentally disturbed with her problems all in her "joy account." It would have been better if she had "removed" them and cashed in on God's compassion, mercy and grace.

Jugete didn't do all that well in our new headquarters. He was always getting out and fighting with stray dogs. One time he fell out of our balcony on the second floor and his back legs were in splints for several weeks. The last straw was his limping home with one eye out, messed up almost beyond recognition. We knew we would have to put him to sleep. Hugh went off to the vet's and shortly later returned—with Jugete. He just couldn't do it. Later, he went again and this time he was successful, but our house was one sad place for a long time after that.

We've always marveled at how God chooses our friends. Union Church, where we were attending, was holding a special fundraiser for CARE Packages that were popular at the time. It was a worthy cause. CARE, founded in 1945, distributed food packages to help survivors of World War II. Later, in addition to emergency relief, the packages were sent out to areas that needed carpentry tools, blankets, school supplies and medicine. What the folks in charge of the fund raiser wanted from us were a few Wycliffe missionaries to do a small skit, in costume, of an ethnic family receiving a CARE package.

Hugh and I and a couple of others got an act together and while we were waiting to go on, I noticed some silk screen tiles and oohed and aahed over them. They were beautiful and being used as door prizes. What I didn't know was that the person who made them, Logan Jones, was standing close by. All of a sudden I heard, "I love you!" and to my surprise this man gave me a great big hug. This was the beginning of a delightful friendship with Logan, his wife Sue, and their son Mark. Sue worked for the American Embassy; Logan was an entrepreneur and had his hand in many things, including making these tiles.

Sue and Logan were such bright spots in our lives. They were loads of fun and a lovely break from communal living that we had at Wycliffe's group headquarters. Sue and Logan are now with the Lord, but they were such a blessing in our lives while in Mexico. They would often come to visit us at the headquarters and bring foodstuffs from the American Embassy like chocolate chips, canned soups and other goodies we couldn't get at the local markets in Mexico. And I remember one time Sue was redecorating their bedroom and gave us their old spread. It was just the color I had been wanting!

. . . .

In 1966, we were privileged to have Margaret and Walter Bennett from Edmonton, Alberta visit us. Shirley Latta (later married to John Kolanchy), a pen pal friend from my childhood whom I later got to know personally, had visited us previously and told her friends the Bennetts they should come down and meet us.

We had a delightful time together as we showed them around Mexico City and also acquainted them with the work Wycliffe Bible Translators was doing in Mexico. They were fascinated when we took them out to visit an Otomi woman who lived in a home made of nothing more than cactus, stumps and a dead tree or two. We developed a delightful friendship over the years with the Bennetts and years later, Karen and I had the opportunity to visit them in their home in Edmonton when we went to visit Shirley and her husband John.

Another interesting friend God chose for us arrived at the Wycliffe headquarters in Mexico in the summer of 1966. Gordon Wetmore, a high school teacher and artist, came to provide a summer program of activities for the Wycliffe kids whose parents worked at the headquarters. Along with the fun games and short trips, he had some of the children sit for portraits. We were fortunate to have him do pastels of both Wendy and David. Later he asked for photographs and did two more fantastic portraits of Lee and Karen.

When he came to Mexico, art was just his hobby. Later, however, he settled with his wife and three daughters in Signal Mountain, Tennessee and went on to not only illustrate several books but he was also included in the seventeenth edition of Who's Who in American Art and did portraits of President Richard Nixon, Dr. & Mrs.

Norman Vincent Peale, author Leon Uris, Princess Grace, His Serene Highness Prince Rainier and His Serene Highness Prince Albert.

When Gordon started out, he painted the portraits of his buddies' girlfriends from wallet photos for $10.00. Several years ago his rates ranged from $4,000 to $10,000 for a single portrait. Checking his website recently, I noticed they start at $15,000! We can truly say, "We knew him when." We so enjoyed the portraits for many years but we gave them to each of the children a few years ago because we wanted to make sure they were in their possession before we passed on.

I can't mention all the wonderful people God has brought into our lives over the years, but I do want to mention our friends George and Marilyn Duff from Mercer Island, Washington. George is the former president of Seattle's Chamber of Commerce. He and his wife are active in several mission groups and were members of our son-in-law Greg's church. When Greg accepted a call as senior pastor of Mercer Island Covenant Church (now known as Evergreen Covenant Church), he put them in touch with us. George and Marilyn used to come down several times a year as they had a place in Seal Beach. Not often do people make fast, good friends in their 70s, but such was the case with George and Marilyn.

Our pastor, Rev. William Sloan, at Ruth Morton when we were commissioned for service with Wycliffe to Mexico in 1957, left after three years and moved on to Yucaipa, California to First Baptist Church. Shortly after he took the pastorate in Yucaipa, California, he invited Hugh to take part in their missionary conference. It was a special joy, since we used our car to transport supplies for the

· ·

missionaries out in the villages, when First Baptist Church informed us they wanted to help us purchase a 1961 Chevrolet Station Wagon. Yucaipa Baptist Church helped us in many ways over the years as they invited us to take part in their missionary conferences, and in 1970, when we moved to Santa Ana, California, the church brought a truckload of furniture for us, but more about that later.

The next great happening in our family was our new family member, Karen Lynn weighing in at seven pounds on March 2, 1967. Yes, she was a surprise. When I suddenly became sick again, I thought I had gastro intestinal flu as several of our friends were sick with it. But my symptoms didn't go away so off we went to the doctor. When he told us I was pregnant, Hugh, completely non-plussed, responded, "How did this happen? I just can't understand it!" The doctor, with tongue in cheek said, "Do you want some literature?" Years later Karen questioned us if she was a "mistake." "How can you be a mistake?" I said. "You're God's gift to us!" And she truly was and is!

It seemed our almost eleven years in Mexico were filled with one medical emergency after another. Karen's birth was no exception. At the time she was due to be delivered, David was in the hospital with severe osteomyelitis in his foot. First we were told, since I was having a Caesarian Section, Hugh could not visit between me and David because of the possibility of transferring germs. Those were a few hectic days, but Karen cooperated and waited to come into this world until David was home from the hospital and all was well. Well, not entirely. When the

....

nurse brought in Karen for me to see my new baby girl for the first time, the doctor came with her.

"I need to warn you that during the Cesarean Section I accidentally cut into Karen's head and you are going to see four stitches," he said, unapologetically. It was only later when another Wycliffe woman was sewn up incorrectly after the birth of her baby that we heard this doctor was an alcoholic. I was just grateful Karen's head cut, while even with her eye, was behind the hairline. Many times I shuddered to think about what would have happened if her head had been turned slightly to the left.

Norma with Karen as a baby   Karen's publicity photo, 2008

In May 1967, Hugh had the privilege of going with Cornell Capa (contributing Life Magazine photographer) and his crew to photograph the dedication of the Lowland Tzeltal New Testament in southern Mexico. Marianna Slocum and Florence Gerdel, the Wycliffe translators, would go on to translate the Highland Tzeltal New

Testament as well as one more New Testament in Colombia before they retired.

This trip would turn out to be a turning point in God's direction for our lives. Hugh had always been interested in photography and writing, and this experience opened the door for him to bring this interest into a full-time reality.

He learned that only fifteen years before Marianna and Florence came to bring the Tzeltals God's Word in their own language, the Tzeltals were feared by the rest of the population in this area. In drunken fury they would kill and rob any hapless traveler or merchant. Now Hugh saw the Bibles distributed and being read under "every tree and shady nook," he wrote in a newsletter. "People gather to study, read, help others to read, and discuss the wonderful new truths that are being made plain to them in their own language."

Hugh's account of the dedication and his photographs were picked up and published by Wycliffe's then in-house publication, "Translation Magazine." Also a photo he took of a close-up of two hands on an open Bible was used on Wycliffe's official stationery for years. And Wycliffe translator and author, Ethel Wallis, told him he should do more.

This inspired Hugh to take a course on journalism from the University of Oklahoma, in which he did very well, and he began to write other articles. Amazingly, everything he wrote that first year he began writing was published, about 18 articles! Hugh went on to do a lot of photography for Wycliffe, not only to illustrate articles, or for books he wrote, but also for Wycliffe's general

....

archives. Many of Hugh's photos were used on their yearly calendars and other coffee table books.

As the summer of 1967 approached, it was evident either we would have to send Wendy stateside to high school, or we would have to move there with her. After attending the Pan American Workshop School and the American School up to the sixth grade, she had completed grades 7-9 at Wycliffe's Mexico City headquarters, where at that time they had a junior high school. Now we felt it was time to get her into a stateside school to prepare for college.

Karen was just a few months old when we started to talk about it and Wendy would cry herself to sleep at night thinking about having to leave the family and especially her new little sister. I had been very ill with this birth, and Wendy, almost 15, was a second mother to Karen. I did have a nurse come in to give Karen her bath every morning, but Wendy learned how to make the formula, and she looked after Karen when she wasn't in school or doing her homework.

I felt strongly my children were given to us by God to bring up for Him and did not want to send Wendy or any of the other children away, so imagine my joy when we were approached by Dr. Dale Kietzman, Wycliffe's Extension (P.R.) Director about being the Regional Director for the eight North Central States. They had found a couple willing to sell Wycliffe what they said was a furnished house in one of the western suburbs of Chicago and Dale felt that since there was an outside building, this would be suitable for a Regional office.

Before we packed up and left however, Wendy's Canadian friend, Linda Brummitt, came for a visit. Hugh took them around Mexico City to see the sights, and also to

. . . .

Manuel Arenas's Bible School (written about in Hugh's book, *Manuel*) with another group of young people who had come down from the States. And our dear friends John and Thelma Scott got in a visit with us as well before we left. We were able to take them to Acapulco for a few days.

Acapulco had become a special place for us during our years in Mexico because we first went there as guests of our Canadian friend, Jack McLellan, a businessman with Dupont in Mexico. In fact, he took us a couple of times along with another missionary couple, Dottie and Ray Masson who were members of the Mexican Indian Mission. When Jack took us, we stayed in a beautiful rented house. Later, when we would go for our vacations, we stayed in the oldest motel in Acapulco that was rather run-down, but it was inexpensive and came with the most fabulous breakfasts you ever ate! Somehow those breakfasts made it worthwhile to put up with the inch-long cockroaches we had in our rooms!

Jack later married Roberta Norman, another Canadian, and we had wonderful times of fellowship together before they moved to the Dupont Headquarters in Wilmington, Delaware.

In August 1967, we broke up our apartment that had been our home for five years after living in the Kettle and the small apartment on Amores Street. Hugh, Wendy and David drove up in the station wagon loaded with some of our household goods. Lee, five, and Karen, five months old, flew with me to Chicago. Jim Hefley, an author we had met in Mexico with his wife Marti and family, met us and took us to their home to wait for Hugh's arrival. (Jim would later help Hugh hone his writing skills.)

We hoped we could be settled into a new home by the start of the school year after Labor Day. Hugh, Wendy and David arrived safely and off we went to look at the house Wycliffe was going to buy for our housing and an office.

"Things are never as they seem" is the old saying, and this house was no exception. The house consisted of one master bedroom on the main floor plus a little alcove where a single bed could fit. There was an apartment upstairs with an outside entrance that would be great for Wycliffe families passing through who needed a place to stay. We, however, had nowhere to put our three children if we put Karen in the little alcove. The outside building would have worked for an office, but the house was situated far away from any post office and in no way was convenient for sending out films, literature and daily mail. The last negative was that the "furnished house" turned out to be one table and a few chairs.

When we mentioned to the owners we were sorry but we didn't think their place was going to be suitable, they became angry with us. They informed us in no uncertain terms they were going to stop their support for a Wycliffe couple. We just happened to know this couple and were friends with them in Mexico. This saddened us, as did our own situation now with nowhere to live, but we felt they had misrepresented their place and bid them good-bye feeling sick about the whole incident! What a way to start a new adventure we felt God was leading us into! It reminded us of our rocky situation years previously when we wondered whether we'd make it into Wycliffe! Once again we were given an opportunity to display His splendor in a difficult situation and learn that God is indeed trustworthy!

The next three weeks we lived with the Hefley family of five. There were six of us and needless to say, although they made us feel welcome, we felt we were imposing. Every day we'd go out looking for suitable houses, but nothing seemed right until one day the realtor took us to a newer lovely split-level three-bedroom home with a screened-in sun porch and an almost completely finished basement with an extra bedroom, sitting room and ample place for an office. Amazingly the owners were selling the house furnished and the price was right. The elderly couple, who were moving into an apartment, generously left things like waste baskets, mops, brooms, and even blankets on a couple of beds. The fridge and stove, washing machine and dryer were also included. We contacted Dale and we were given the okay to buy it in Wycliffe's name and were able to move in on Labor Day weekend in time for Lee to begin Kindergarten at a school just a block away, David to enter Jr. High and Wendy to begin her sophomore year in high school. Our God is an awesome God! And we also were so grateful to the Hefleys who went over and beyond the call of duty having us live with them for three weeks! They have gone on to glory but they were still our friends at the end! Imagine that!

Along with arranging speaking engagements for Wycliffe members home on furlough, sending out Wycliffe films to churches and cleaning them when they were returned, we wrote numerous letters for those interested in Wycliffe and took many speaking engagements ourselves. We also had many Wycliffe people stay with us, mostly men, it seemed. Wendy would often have to give up her bed as her bedroom became the guest room. In fact, one day she commented that, like her father, she was going to write her own book with the title, "Men Who Have Slept in my Bed." It probably would have sold better than Hugh's missionary books!

Hugh continued to write and started his first book, *Manuel*, at Ethel Wallis's suggestion. She had been asked to write Manuel Arenas's story, "but I think you're ready to write a book," she said to Hugh. "I think you should be the one to do this."

Hugh had been thinking about writing a book on Herman Aschmann translator to the Totonacs, Manuel's language group, but he had also interviewed Manuel for an article, so with some beginning material, he began and completed his first book our second year in Buffalo Grove, Illinois, where our new house was situated.

Coming to the United States after ten and a half years in Mexico was an adjustment for us all. But for five-year-old Lee, having T.V. for the first time in his life was exciting. He wanted to watch everything, but I was selective, of course, especially on Saturday morning with what I felt were violent cartoons. However, there was one program I really liked, and Lee did, too. It was Romper Room hosted by Mary Carol Reilly. I was so grateful for that program, I wrote a thank you letter to Mary Carol telling her we had just come from Mexico and I appreciated her informative and instructive program for children.

About two weeks later I received a call from her. I was naturally surprised! I didn't think T.V. personalities just called people out of the blue and chatted with them like old friends. She wanted to know what we were doing in Mexico, why we were now in the U.S., and would Lee like to be a guest on her program? I said I was overwhelmed she would invite him and we made arrangements for the date he would come.

The conversation then shifted to talking about Mexico and she mentioned how she loved Mexican food. On the spur of the moment I asked her if she'd like to come for a Mexican dinner, and she gave an immediate, "Yes!"

We discovered she was a former nun and she said her priest and nun friends would love to meet us. So I invited them over for an evening, and we did have a stimulating time. The result of that was an invitation to come and share my faith at a weekend retreat for senior high school girls from parochial schools in the Chicago area. But first I had to be checked out by the priests running the program.

Not having had much to do with priests and nuns, in fact, nil, on the appointed day I went with butterflies in my stomach and knees knocking. I decided, however, I wasn't going to beat about the bush. I would state clearly my relationship to Jesus Christ.

The meeting was in Chicago and as I walked into this room, there, sitting in a circle, were about 15 priests. They wanted to hear what I would be sharing with the girls. I took a deep breath and began, using Scripture to back up my points about my faith not being the keeping of rules or rituals but rather a growing relationship with Jesus Christ.

At one point one of the priests interrupted me and said, "Are you going to be using Scripture?"

"Yes," I said, feeling that perhaps this would be the end of our conversation. But his answer surprised me.

"Good!" he thundered. "We need to use more Scripture at our retreats." I could tell they were pleased as they nodded their heads. And yes, I passed muster!

We met in the Holy Spirit Convent in Techny, Illinois from a Friday to a Monday morning. I admit I probably had more prejudice against them than they had against me as a Protestant. I suppose I thought I had an edge when it came to "correct" doctrine, but I was pleasantly surprised with the theme of the retreat. The girls were reminded that when they were baptized as infants, someone else had said "yes," for them. Now that they were high school seniors, it was time for them to make their own decision about following Christ. The whole weekend was geared to helping them understand what making a personal commitment to Christ was all about.

I thought my role in the weekend would just be to share my faith journey. However, since they were short one table leader, they asked if I'd be willing to lead a table of girls. I was happy to.

This weekend was a requirement for the girls to graduate and most showed interest in the teaching and activities. Most, that is, except for four African American girls. I had one of the four at my table. She had taken the name "Tabula" although her given name was Sandra. It was obvious she did not want to be there.

I was determined to reach Tabula and went out of my way to show interest in her. She seemed to warm up to me and one day, when I had on purple dangly earrings that matched my purple dress, she complimented me on them. I felt I was getting somewhere.

I gave my testimony and was told when I was finished to take all the girls to the chapel and teach them conversational prayer, since most of the prayers they prayed were rote. I was delighted to note that the chapel was devoid of images. There were no chairs. Just one tall candle and a large rock with an open Bible on it.

The girls gathered. Some sat; others kneeled. I was just about to begin praying when they started in without letting me get a word out. I still remember how refreshing their prayers were. Especially one girl who began, "O God, you know how stubborn and independent I am. I like to do things my own way. But the next time I get going on something without checking in with You, please give me a good swift kick in the butt!"

There were other spontaneous prayers. They came one after another. The room was electric with confessions and praise and I was delighted to be a bystander.

For our last activity we were to make a collage depicting friendship and acceptance. Each table had a big piece of poster board and a pile of magazines and we were to cut out illustrations of our theme. Everyone entered in enthusiastically, even Tabula. She found a cute picture of a little black boy and girl hugging and underneath was the caption, "What good is a kiss without a hug."

Our last activity was the celebration of the Mass. I once again needed to be questioned about my thoughts on the subject. I told them that for me Communion, as I called it, was a remembrance of Christ's sacrifice on my behalf. The priests and nuns talked about that for a while, but they finally decided it was okay for me to partake of the Eucharist as a memorial.

I learned later that they believed I was the first Protestant in Illinois to have ever been invited to join in a Catholic Mass. It was a special moment for me and the joy of it was evident. After the service, a couple of the priests gave me a big hug and one of the nuns grabbed me and we danced down the hall. Later I said if someone had told me that one day I would be in a convent being hugged by priests and dancing down the hall with a nun, I'd have told them they were crazy!

TEC, Holy Spirit Center   TEC # HS 40
Techny, Illinois 60082   Mar. 29-31, '69

Weekend conference at Holy Spirit Convent. That's me second from right in the front row. Tabula, in dark shirt, is two left of the second nun to the left, just above girl with striped shirt and long blond hair.

Tabula had not come to the service and I was heartsick. I knew of only one thing to do. My earrings had been a gift from a friend, but I decided I would see where Tabula was and give the earrings to her as a gift. I wrote a little note saying I knew she had suffered prejudice, but I hoped she would accept the earrings as one little step to make things right from a friend who loved her.

I went up to the dorm where the girls slept and looked around the big room. I spied Tabula feigning sleep, tried to arouse her, but she wouldn't respond. I left the little bag with the earrings on her bedside table and went back down to our activity room where we would have our final goodbyes.

All the girls and leaders joined hands and we sang several of the songs we had learned that weekend. I still remember the words of one of the songs:

> To be alive and feeling free
> And to have everyone in our family,
> To be alive, in every way,
> Oh, how great it is, to be alive!

We were on the last song and I was praying Tabula would show up, as much for her sake as mine. There was a rustle at the door. All heads turned, and there she was! She crossed through the center of the circle and came over to where I was. She had on the earrings! With a kiss and a hug, and said, "What good is a kiss without a hug." What a precious moment!

When we got back to our tables, people were writing in each other's notebooks and Tabula asked for mine. I read it after she had left for home with the others.

> Dearest Norma,
>
>   Words can't express my attitude on life now. At first, I didn't want to accept you or the Church. I didn't realize until today that I've been going along all the time saying I wasn't prejudiced when now I know I was. When I received your lovely earrings,

you made me want to kill myself because time has gone by and I have hurt many people. I didn't want to accept the Church because it is made up of a white society who are the ones who first converted the Africans to turn to God. By these means their lands as well as themselves were taken. They had no future. This is the reason why I no longer wanted to be a part of the Church. I did not want my people to be tricked again because we have so very little. The Bible, as you know, is so very powerful and I didn't want to be led away, not wanting to fall into its so-called trap.

I see now, after several hours of praying as well as crying, that no matter what color, we cannot survive without God.

In my prayers I ask God to give me strength to know the differences, which are so minute, in each of us, and to realize that Christ really is God's Son, human as well as God. You gave me faith. Don't forget me. (Signed) Tabula.

Tabula wrote her thoughts in pencil and over the years her letter has faded, but I'm so glad I kept it so I could share it with you. We kept in touch for a while. She sent me her grad picture and on the back she wrote, "Well, Norma, here I am graduating in a cap and gown. There's a big difference, isn't there? Love, Sandy." I was thrilled to see she was back using her given name and indeed there was a difference in her face. I was sorry to have lost touch with her but I know we shall meet again in a "better place."

10

Furlough, U.S. Residency, New Offices, Children's Faith

While the adjustment to being back in the U.S. was difficult for us all, it was hardest for Hugh. You might say he had an identity crisis. He didn't feel he could call himself a writer yet, and he missed Mexico so much, he wanted to go back. We did go back for the summer and came back to Bufffalo Grove, Illinois for our second year, but Hugh was not happy. In his mind, in June we would take a two-month furlough in Vancouver, leave Wendy with friends, and go back to Mexico. I, in no way, was in agreement, but to keep the peace, after stating how I felt, went along with him. I felt sorry for Wendy who already had been in two high schools in two countries, and now she was about to complete her senior year in Canada, a third country and a third high school.

We left Buffalo Grove and drove to Vancouver the summer of 1969. We were able to stay in Lillian Hamilton's home, another friend from Ruth Morton Baptist Church, who was away for the summer, and then Hugh was insistent we return to Mexico. Once again we called on our friends, John and Thelma Scott, to help us out and keep Wendy for the year.

The night before we were to travel back to Mexico, we received a call from, Phil Chiddell, longtime friend.

"Hugh," he said, "we thought you'd like to know Anne and I have decided to go over to Salt Spring Island for a year. A position has opened up for me and if you'd like to rent our house for the year, it's available to you for $125.00 a month. We're leaving it furnished because the place where we'll be staying is furnished."

It seemed almost too good to be true! I was ecstatic and just whooped and hollered and praised the Lord. Phil knew we had talked about taking a year's furlough but didn't feel we would ever find a place we could afford. What he didn't know, however, was that when I was begging Hugh to stay, we talked about how much we could afford for rent, and Hugh had said, "About one hundred twenty-five a month, and how are we going to find a place at that price?" Phil had not heard us quote that figure. I just knew God had worked another miracle for us.

But Hugh had his mind set on getting back to Mexico and turned him down. I decided I would be quiet for a change and prayed God would help Hugh to see the value of our being with Wendy for her senior year, and also giving me the joy of being around my dear mother whom I hadn't seen much in the last 12 years. We drove off the next morning to leave Wendy at the Scotts, and I can still see in my mind's eye the look on Wendy's face. It was frantic and wet with tears as she waved good-bye.

I sat in the back seat of the car with Lee and Karen. David was up front with Hugh and no one said hardly anything all the way to Seattle. We had stopped in Bellevue to see our friends Dan and Bev O'Brien who were

. . . .

now on leave from Mexico helping Dan's father with his restaurant, "O'Brien's Turkey House" (later called "O'Brien's Turkey Manor), but they weren't home. We then drove toward Steven's Pass. Funny, as we were driving it seemed all the motels were on the other side of the freeway, so when we found a turnaround, we crossed over and headed back to a motel we had just passed.

In my mind I thought, *O Lord, at least we're pointed in the right direction for going back. Please take us back. I don't feel good about this. I feel we are disobeying You.*

We settled in for the night and in the morning, when Hugh still insisted on going on, I just sat in the back praying my heart out.

We didn't go too far before Hugh saw a turnaround and pulled in. And then he had a battle with himself going forward and backward trying to decide what to do. David sank down into the front seat, as if to hide, and said, "I can't believe this!"

Finally, in obvious agony, Hugh said, "I'll tell you what. We'll go ahead and find a phone and call Wendy. If she still wants us to come back, we will."

Even as I write this, I remember my sigh of relief. I knew Wendy would want us to come back. God had answered my earnest pleadings!

When I called Wendy and said, "Would you like us to come back?" there was a pause, and then she said, "You would do that for me?" "Yes," I said. "We'll stop at the O'Brien's on the way up and pick you up later today." Hugh then called the Chiddells to see if the house was still available. It was!

This time when we stopped at the O'Brien's they were home, and they affirmed us in our decision to spend a

. . . .

year's furlough in Vancouver, especially since we had a place to stay. After a short visit we were on our way, and when we arrived to pick up Wendy, there were many tears of joy.

We settled into Chiddell's home on E. 47th Ave. in South Vancouver, not too far from our former home. Wendy and David were enrolled in John Oliver High School, my alma mater—David as a Freshman; Wendy as a Senior. Lee entered the second grade. David immediately got involved in sports, both track and football, and made a good adjustment. The coach hated to see him leave when our year was over.

Wendy needed only one more credit to graduate had we stayed in Illinois, so it was upsetting for her to discover she needed seven heavy subjects to graduate from a Canadian school. She had so much homework that year there were times she stayed home to get her assignments done. It was a difficult year for her, but great preparation for college!

Not as outgoing as David, Wendy nevertheless determined to make the best of this year. The first day she walked into the lunchroom at John Oliver, she spied a table of what looked like "nice" girls and slowly walked over and introduced herself. Imagine her delight when the group of girls turned out to be Christians from a Mennonite Brethren church. They became her best friends that year. When graduation rolled around, none of the girls, including Wendy, knew how to dance, but they were determined to learn so they could have the first dance with their fathers. And they all did!

. . . .

The summer of 1969 when we arrived in Vancouver, we began a tradition that lasted twenty-seven summers—spending a week or ten days at Thetis Island, one of the Gulf Islands off the coast of Vancouver, B.C., as a guest of our friend, Neil McKay, in his waterfront A-frame cabin.

Dubbed by Karen, "Big Rock," this huge outcropping stood like a sentinel in front of Neil McKay's A-frame cabin on Thetis Island. Here Lee is in his favorite place to read a book

It was a modest cabin, but we always felt we had a millionaire's holiday at the most beautiful place in the world. Fishing was wonderful in those early years and meeting Ken and Ruth Smith and Fred and Marg Linsey, who spent summers in their lovely waterfront homes only a few yards away, was a wonderful blessing. Each year we looked forward to seeing them, our "summertime friends." We made other "summertime friends," too. Anne and Stan Wilbee and Blake and Bridget Dickens, both of whom had summer homes on Thetis Island, and it was always fun when our vacations coincided with them being there as well. Some summers we even got to stay in

Hugh catches our supper…an early evening ritual in the early days

Smith's or Linsey's lovely homes when Neil's cabin was occupied.

Karen was with us at Thetis Island for about half of the twenty-seven years. Lee less than that as he began working summers. We are indebted to Neil for many years of inestimable joy in God's beautiful creation, to say nothing of all those wonderful salmon feasts!

The year 1969-1970 was probably the most difficult of Wendy's life. For Hugh, however, it was "the best Christmas of my life. Fleming Revel informed me they were going to publish my book!" This began Hugh on the

. . . .

road to becoming Wycliffe's "Author and Photographer-at-large" but at that time, he still had his heart set on getting back to Mexico.

In May 1970, while still in Vancouver, Hugh also made his first trip of many to gather photos and story material for Wycliffe publications. In this case, it was to Ghana, West Africa to take colored slides for a film strip. Because Wycliffe receives all royalties from Hugh's books, Hugh's film and trip expenses were always paid by Wycliffe. Sometimes it was hard to explain to people that this was our assignment just as much as someone out in an ethnic region translating the Scriptures, or a teacher, nurse, buyer, typist or electrician who was a Wycliffe member.

And then the school year was finished and Hugh was anxious to get started south once more. After a week at Thetis Island for our second year, we left Wendy with Hugh's mother. She had a job at the Vancouver General Hospital as a cleaning lady for the summer, thanks to a friend from Main Street Gospel Hall, Lorene Campbell, and our friends Joe and Audrey Renny from Ruth Morton Baptist Church, offered to take her to Seattle Pacific College (now University) at the end of September where she would begin her college career.

David, Lee and Karen were with us, and as we drove down, I was sick at heart that we had David scheduled to go to the Wycliffe's children's home in Oklahoma City for the last three years of his high school. I asked God, that if it was His will, He would work it out for us to stay in Santa Ana where Wycliffe's International Headquarters was then located.

. . . .

Our first stop on reaching Santa Ana was an appointment with our good friend, the Executive Director of the Summer Institute of Linguistics and Wycliffe Bible Translators (SIL/WBT), Dr. Benjamin (Ben) Elson (he was our director in Mexico for some of the years we were there and in 1965 was appointed Deputy General Director for North America. He held the title of Wycliffe's Executive Director of SIL/WBT from 1966-1975). After hearing about our furlough year and Hugh's success in getting his book, *Manuel* published along with several other articles, Ben suggested perhaps we should think about staying in Santa Ana and writing full time. It was a tough sell for Hugh as this was not what he wanted to hear. However, knowing my feelings about not wanting to send David away, he said we would stay if we could find a place to rent at a price we could afford—a tall order because our monthly support was still very low and with Wendy in a private college, we didn't have two extra pennies to rub together.

As we were sitting in his office, Ben called Dottie Brown, a realtor, friend of Wycliffe, and member of Trinity Presbyterian Church where Ben and his wife Adelle attended, and later we discovered she suggested a vacant home in a good area at a fair price. We didn't know what Dottie was saying to Ben at the time, of course, but Hugh said later, as Ben talked, something inside him said this was going to be our home.

Dottie picked us up and showed us the three-bedroom home with a small yard and while we liked it, I felt we should look at a few more homes before we made our decision. It turned out this first property, at 1309 N. Linwood Avenue in Santa Ana, was the one we liked best.

The selling price was $29,000.00. The house had been empty for some time and Dottie felt the woman would be willing to come down a little more. There was one problem. We needed $500.00 to make an offer, but we had used all our savings for Wendy's college tuition. Further, because we were in transit, we had not received a Wycliffe check for a couple of months from monies that had come in from donors. We had to tell Dottie we didn't have $500.00 to make our offer. "No problem," said Dottie, "just write me a promissory note." We did, and the seller accepted our offer of $26,000.00!

Our home at 1309 N. Linwood Ave., Santa Ana, California, 92701.
To the left is the two-story garage where our offices are located

However, there was yet another hurdle. In order to qualify for a loan, we had to come up with more money for the down payment because we had only received $9,000.00 the year before and with being "faith" missionaries, we didn't have a steady income. The amount we needed for the down payment was $6000.00. We still had $1500.00 in bonds for Wendy's next semester. We cashed these in along with an insurance policy. First Baptist in Yucaipa sent us a check for $800.00. Hugh's mother loaned us $1000.00, as did Wycliffe (we paid back these loans at $25.00 a month). The balance, that included the $500.00 to Dottie to pay off the promissory note, we made up with our two-month check that finally caught up with us. This left us with practically nothing to live on for the next month and because the owner had agreed to the lower price, she would not pay for the termite tenting. Dottie Brown came to the rescue again and not only paid for the termite tenting, she also bought us a small second-hand fridge. God uses people to provide needs and He certainly has used Dottie and Bill in our lives.

We were all set to move in, but we didn't have a stick of furniture. Fortunately we had a built-in oven and range. And that's when First Baptist Church in Yucaipa came to our rescue again. When we told Rev. Sloan about our dilemma, that first week they came with a truckload of used furniture—table and chairs, sofa, beds, a small black and white T.V., a coffee table, lamp and more. We went out shopping at Goodwill and found a couple of bedside tables—one for $2.00, the other for $1.50. We used them for years, and when we could replace them, Karen used them in her rented condo before she was married. Our neighbors across the street, Gordon and Marilyn Hendry, who introduced us to Trinity Presbyterian Church, told us about their friend Betty Thompson who was getting rid of two chests of drawers, so we went over and picked them up. Finally we were getting some semblance of order with our family of five now that Wendy was away at college. We had left Vancouver with only a six-foot trailer filled

· ·

with our personal possessions, books and some household goods, but in no time, it seemed we would need a moving van if we were to move again!

Over the years people gave us other furniture and we found inexpensive pieces ourselves. We've been able to replace the original furniture and we are most grateful for all we have. Our 1400 square foot home was only thirteen years old when we moved in. We've now been here 50 years! When all the children were living at home, it was somewhat crowded, but now it is most adequate.

In November 1986, when Trinity's Mission Committee called and said they had $5,000.00 extra in their budget to give us toward building an office over our garage, we hardly knew what to say. Kristi, Dave's wife, was on the Missions Committee at that time and had told them that Hugh was working in an unheated and un-air-conditioned, unfinished garage and I was working in our dining room. The only catch was that the money had to be used before the end of the year, two months away, or it would go back into the general fund. My memory fails me regarding the details, but in a February 1987 newsletter with photos of our offices, we wrote:

> We're in business! Thank you for praying. And we want to thank the Missions Committee at Trinity Presbyterian Church and King's Class for their gifts of time, money and labor. Special thanks to Bill Brown for overseeing the construction; to Dave Solomon for directing the project, and to Wayne West for his month-long labor in building book shelves, entry ways and donating and putting in a beautiful hardwood entrance door. What a gift of love! Pray we will be good stewards of this

....

expanded working space and that our writing ministry with Wycliffe will bring honor and glory to God.

So many were involved in this project, I hesitate naming names. There were over twenty volunteers from our adult Sunday School class, including Hugh and Lynn Galt. Lynn sewed a beautiful curtain for the bathroom window and they bought and installed the mini-blinds. Dick and Karen Titus, then Trinity members, provided a heat pump and air conditioning unit. On December 14, we held a big celebration and dedicated the office. But now I am ahead of myself again. Back to 1971.

While we were adjusting to Southern California, Wendy was not adjusting to Seattle Pacific College. She wanted to

come home. Our letters and calls flowed back and forth constantly, but Wendy kept saying she wanted to leave. About this time our friends Dan and Bev O'Brien called Wendy, now managing their Turkey House Manor in Arlington, Washington, and asked if she wanted to come to their place for the weekend. Wendy said later that if they hadn't called, she was

Front: Lee, Norma, Karen
Back: Hugh, Dave, Wendy

determined to go back up to Canada and stay with either my parents or Hugh's.

This began a weekly affair for Wendy as she began to work weekends in their restaurant and it was a lifesaver in keeping her at her studies. That and the fact that I had told her she couldn't come home! There wasn't room. Unless, of course, she wanted her four-year-old sister for a roommate. It was one of the hardest things I've ever said to my children, and while true, I hoped the shock of it would make her realize she would have to stay where she was.

When she came home for Christmas and was doing much better, I told her I had kept all her letters because I knew she'd come around. "Well, I kept yours, too," said Wendy, "because I would go over them and read all the good stuff you were saying in them."

"Hey," I responded, "let's put the letters in a book. Maybe they would help other kids struggling with being away from home for the first time." And that's just what we did. I signed a contract with Fleming H. Revell Company, who had published Hugh's first book, *Manuel*, and in 1971 my book came out under the title, *Please Can I Come Home? No You Can't Come Home!*

We were still uncertain how long we were going to be in Santa Ana. We felt at least we should stay here until David finished high school. It was a wise decision. David had so many questionings about Christianity and his own faith. Hugh sometimes would stay up until one and two in the morning listening, answering David's deep, probing questions and explaining biblical truths. Many times we've talked about how important it was to be with David through those high school years. If we had sent him off to Wycliffe's children's home in Oklahoma, the house parents couldn't have taken that much time with him with so many other missionary kids in the home.

Several other good things resulted for David with our being here in Santa Ana. He was able to go on several mission trips with the youth group. He was a star football player throughout his years at Santa Ana High School and won a four-year football scholarship to Baylor University in Waco, Texas, a wonderful financial help for us. Kristi Robbins, whom he met in high school, would become his wife. He became good friends with Dennis Stamps and in their senior year they would go off weekly to a Bible study with Chuck Smith at Calvary Chapel. So with Hugh helping him to settle his faith questions and Chuck Smith grounding him in the Word, it was much easier to send him off across the country to Baylor University after his senior year of high school knowing he was firmly grounded in his faith.

As for "Little Lee," he was no longer little and he, too, was getting interested in football at Willard Jr. High. It also became evident God had given him a good brain. "He not only can do the math," his teacher said at a parent-teacher conference, "he understands how it works!"

He won several awards when he graduated from Willard and went on to Santa Ana High School where he was enrolled in the GATE program, an accelerated program for advanced students. He continued to play football in High School, was awarded the top Scholar-Athlete Award, and was valedictorian when he graduated.

During his high school and college summers, he worked with Wayne West, handyman and painter, as his helper. It was great preparation for his own house after he was married, but with Wayne paying him $10.00 an hour, it was a wonderful help for his own expenses.

As for Karen, with Wendy and David away at college, she decided she didn't want to grow up. "I don't want to be a big sister like Wendy," she said one day, "'cause you have to go away." With almost 15 years between her and Wendy, ten between David, and five between Lee, she shed a lot of tears with their comings and goings.

But there was one joy in her life, and that was her beagle, "Freckles." Our next door neighbor brought Freckles over one day in December 1971. It was the runt of the litter but whether she was a thoroughbred or a mongrel, I was not anxious to have a dog as we have such a small back yard.

However, I knew Karen needed companionship, so I reluctantly gave in. And for the next thirteen years I felt Freckles had to be the worst dog in the world and many times I said, with tongue-in-cheek, "That dog makes me lose my sanctification!"

How Karen loved that dog! She slept at the foot of her bed under the covers, even though I'd drag her out. Not Karen, but Freckles! Like Wendy, Karen would dress up Freckles and she complied. But that dog was the personification of sin! When we'd go out for an evening, I'd try to barricade her in the kitchen

. . . .

and dining area where she could get in and out of her doggie door, but she always found ways to get into the living room and bedrooms, wetting the beds and snorting under the sofa cushions to also "moisten" them.

She chewed her way out of the enclosed yard by eating through the wooden gate many times and we'd have to go looking for her. Often she was just sitting as pretty as you please directly across the street on Hendry's porch. And she chewed on shoes, slippers, Karen's Barbie dolls and anything else she fancied. Need I say more? Yes, eventually she too had to be put to sleep and this time David did the duty, and Hugh and I rejoiced while Karen cried herself to sleep. What we don't put up with for our children!

I felt Karen needed some human playmates as well, and enrolled her in a nearby United Methodist preschool where she met Janet Wylie. I met Janet's mother Barbara, and because we were both older mothers, we had a lot in common and became good friends. Another bonus was that Barbara and her husband Jim also attended the same church as us.

Karen had a delightful way of expressing herself, making up words if need be. For instance, the knots in her long hair she called "stregs," and when she learned to clean fish when we had our vacations at Thetis, she dubbed the innards, "ginnards." In 1972, when she was five, she answered the phone and called Hugh saying, "It's the man who speaks in church." It was George Munzing, our beloved pastor. I guess she recognized his voice. Later I told her that he was called, "pastor," or "preacher" because he talks about God. "Boy," she said, "he really must be a Christian then...badly!" (Translation: "He really

· ·

must be a good Christian!") One Sunday morning she remarked, "When people don't go to church, does the devil say 'Hip hip hooray?"

We called Karen "The child of our senility" because we were almost 37 when she was born. One good thing about having a child in one's later years, after three others, is that you start to get the hang of parenting. We were so delighted many times by her spontaneous love for God and her delightful inquiring mind. Like asking us one day, "Does God have a dog?" Another day as Dave went out the door, she yelled after him, "Be sure to tell people about God!" I don't remember where Dave was going at the time, but Karen kept wondering, after he left, if he was doing a good job telling people God loved them. I assured her he probably was, so she finally seemed satisfied and said, "Oh goody!" and went off to play.

Karen's delight in God made me realize she was ready to understand about asking Jesus into her life. I still remember sitting down on our raised fireplace hearth in the dining room and going through a "Wordless Book" with her. I believe she was five years old.

There were no words, just four colored pages of gold, black, red, and white, with a green cover. We first looked at the gold page and I explained that this reminded us of heaven, a place where God lives and He wants us all to come and live with Him. Karen said, "That's where I want to go." "Me, too," I said.

Then we looked at the black page and I said, "This is how the bad things we do look to God. It's called sin. You know, like telling lies and disobeying and saying *no* when I want you to do something. And Jesus says, 'No sin can come into my Heaven.'"

. . . .

Next I opened to the red page and told her that the Bible tells us that God had a good plan. He loved us so much He sent Someone to pay for all the bad things we've done. That Someone was his only Son Jesus and he sent Him to die on the cross. The red stands for the blood that came out of his hands and feet when they nailed Him to the cross. But He didn't stay dead. He came alive again and now He's in Heaven. And if you believe that Jesus is God's Son and that He died for your sins, you can be forgiven for the bad things you do and go to be with Him when you die.

"I believe that," she said, and almost in the same breath asked, "What does the white page mean?"

"Well, that means because Jesus died for our sins, all that blackness, our sins, are now white. We're clean, if we believe what the Bible says and ask Him to come into our lives so He can help us to live pleasing to Him."

"I want to do that," said Karen.

"Do you want to pray and ask Jesus to forgive your sin and come into your heart?" I asked, sensing she understood and was ready.

"Yes," said Karen, looking at me like I should already know that.

"Well let's pray then," I said. "You say the words after me. Dear Jesus, thank you for dying for my sin, please come into my heart. I want to go to heaven to be with You. Thank you! In Jesus name, Amen."

I can't remember if those were the exact words, but Karen prayed and I knew she understood what she was doing. We talked about how we will still do wrong things sometimes but when we ask Jesus to forgive us, He will. I explained the green cover stood for growing in our faith

· ·

and getting to know Jesus better and doing what pleases Him.   We continued to pray nightly and she grew in her understanding of how to pray and learned about Jesus as we had nightly Bible stories.   She understood how to live for God as she observed us and went to Sunday School, church and had camp experiences.   I'm so grateful for the good Sunday School teachers and Jr. and Sr. high teachers she had at Trinity.

Lee, at ten, was also spiritually tender.   He was the only one of our children who at age five asked Jesus into his heart on his own while he was in Sunday School.   We were living in Buffalo Grove, Illinois in 1967 and attending Arlington Heights Baptist Church.   When he came out of his Sunday School class, he quietly said, "Know what I did today?"

"What?" I asked.

"I asked Jesus into my heart."   I wondered if he really knew what he had done, but that night I knew he did.   He loved to put all his stuffed animals around his head when he went to sleep and after praying with him and kissing him goodnight, I walked down the hall.   Before I got to the living room to sit down, I heard him talking out loud, so I tip-toed back to see what was going on.   He was in the middle of telling his little stuffed friends that he had asked Jesus into his heart that morning and now one day he was going to be in heaven with Jesus.

One night he asked to talk to me, so we talked in bed for half an hour.   This was special as he had not asked to do this for several years.   He was five years old when we moved to Buffalo Grove, Illinois, and every night he'd ask me to lie down with him so we could talk and he'd tell me everything he did that day. It got to be such a habit I was worried he'd never outgrow it! If Hugh and I went out for the evening, Wendy had the task of lying down beside him, and if she thought he was taking too long to go to sleep and try to sneak out, he would get very upset.

Now this night I wondered what he wanted to talk about. "Can you tell me about how you and Dad accepted the Lord?" he said. What a precious experience that was!

At Christmas that year, Lee was in a play at school. He needed a toy soldier costume and every time I came up with something that would go with the outfit, like a tall fringed hat I made out of a filing folder and strips of tissue paper cut in fringes, he'd say, "Jesus is so good to help us."

Dave, too, at seventeen in 1972, was growing in his faith and wanting to please the Lord. His serious study of the Word was a joy to our hearts.   And Wendy, was continuing to grow in her faith at Seattle Pacific College where she was majoring in French and Education. She, by the way, was finally happy and more contented. Could be

because a certain young man had come into her life. This particular relationship lasted three years, and later another relationship lasted two years before Mr. Right came along.

I praise God that all four children grew in their faith as they grew. They married Christian spouses and have brought up their children to know and love God. All eleven grandchildren have invited

Christ into their lives, and now we pray for Great Grandson Luke David, who has already been dedicated to the Lord, and those who are yet to be born. My earnest daily prayer has been for us all to take God seriously and follow Him wholeheartedly. May we all indeed be "oaks of righteousness for the display of His splendor."

11

Victories, Bible Studies
and Children's Updates

When we were in Mexico, and before we went in 1957, I never thought much about what we had or didn't have. It seemed to me that most of our friends were at the same economic level as we were.   But when we came to Santa Ana in 1970, it was a different story.   Our new friends lived in wealthy Orange County and I've already alluded to feeling at times like a charity case.   When we were invited for dinner to a beautiful home, I would come home depressed.

I did entertain many Wycliffe people who were in this area, and some of our closest friends still talk about our "split-level" dining.   The table we were given only seated six, and since we were five—six when Wendy came home—I had to set up a card table at the end of our table and sit Karen and Lee up at the bar.   The card table was lower than the main table, hence the "split-level!"

Our sofas didn't match.   I had mismatched lamps, and the dark indoor-outdoor carpet didn't help.   I couldn't color coordinate my bathrooms or bedrooms.   In a word, my artistic sense had to be buried.   I was discontented, embarrassed and unhappy.   Unhappy because of what I didn't have and because I knew I had a bad attitude. Since

I couldn't change things, there was only one thing left to do. *I* had to change.

One day when I was battling with my discontented self, I read Luke 17:11-19 where Jesus wanted to know where the other nine lepers were He had healed. Only one came back to thank Him and He said, "Were not all cleansed? Where are the other nine? Was no one found to return and give praise to God...?"

Obviously, Jesus likes thankfulness! And I knew the Apostle Paul's letters to the churches emphasized the importance of thankfulness.

As I wrestled with this problem, I knew I needed to ask God's help. I began in the dining room praying out loud, "Father, I thank You for this dining room, for the table and chairs and the two stools. These are your gifts to us and I ask Your forgiveness for thinking they aren't good enough."

I walked into the living room and thanked Him for something to sit on, that we had light and drapes (though well-worn!) to keep out the sun and night.

Then it was to the kitchen, the two bathrooms and three bedrooms. As I thanked God for the house and rooms and everything in them, I found my joy returning. I still had a way to go with embarrassment at times, but little by little we were able to get more furniture and decorate more tastefully and that helped.

Then one day I learned that interior decorating did not necessarily mean beautiful furniture and expensive bric-a-brac.

It was Easter and Hugh was on one of his six-week trips to gather material for a Wycliffe book. I had a call from a friend in Huntington Beach who asked if I'd be willing to meet a woman in her complex who wanted to go to a Presbyterian Church service for Easter.

"Of course," I said. "I'll meet her in the patio at 10:45. Can you describe her so I know who to look for?"

"She's short," she said, "and pretty. She's a former movie star and was a double for Debbie Reynolds. You can't miss her!"

I knew what she meant about not missing her when she arrived. She was dressed to the nines, a "classy woman."

We greeted each other and went into the sanctuary. All was well until our pastor, Rev. George Munzing started his sermon. She was obviously agitated and at one point put her hands over her ears. I didn't know what to think. As we walked out, however, I felt prompted to ask her if she'd like to come home with me for lunch. I wondered what David, Lee and Karen would think, but before I left for church that morning, I had put a seven-bone roast (the least expensive of all beef cuts!) in my electric fry pan with carrots and potatoes, a package of Lipton Onion Soup and a bit of water poured over the whole thing. It would not be fancy, but I knew it would be tasty.

As we walked through our door into the living room, I felt, in a way, it was a victory for me to ask her and not be overly concerned about my house and table settings. All I had were cast-off square, multi-colored, thick plastic dishes from another missionary. And if another missionary doesn't want them, you know they have to be pretty bad!

The colors were bilious—maroon, gray, chartreuse and dark purple. True! We saw a set some years later in the B.C. Provincial Museum in Victoria, B.C., Canada. They were listed as a relic from the 1940s!

My guest followed me into the kitchen, walked into the dining room, and sat down on one of the chairs by the table. "What a lovely place you have," she said, as she looked around the room. Then, as I was putting the finishing touches on the meal, she said, "Oh, I know what it is. It's love I feel!"

I think that is probably the nicest compliment I've ever received in all our years in this home, even now tastefully, if modestly, decorated. And I learned that day that it isn't the inanimate things we put into our house that make it a home. It's an *emotion* — love!

I interacted with this new friend during the six weeks Hugh was gone. I discovered she was into Edgar Cayce's teaching on reincarnation. Perhaps this is why God's truth hurt her ears. Every time I tried to bring up anything about my Christian faith, she'd get the most painful headache and that would be the end of our conversation. I helped her with a garage sale. And when she asked me to go with her to Palm Springs to buy a new home, I went.

I tried on the way home to talk to her again about her need for Christ as she was such an unhappy person, but the car kept stalling. We got off the freeway and had a garage mechanic drive it to see if he could fix the problem, but it never stalled for him! When we got to our place, she didn't want to turn off the motor because she was afraid the motor might die and she wouldn't get it started again. She called me once after that and I never heard from her again. I feel God gave her an opportunity to turn away from darkness into light, but she refused.

I had never heard of Bible Study Fellowship (BSF), but when it came to Trinity I decided to attend. We would

. . . .

have a lecture on the passage we were studying, then meet with a discussion leader to discuss the questions we had been given the week before, and then as we left, we were given notes and questions for the next week.

It was in-depth wonderful material written by a Miss A. Wetherell Johnson, former missionary to China. I still remember learning the phrase from her notes, "Nothing is wasted with God" and have experienced this truth over and over again on my life's journey.

One precious memory of this study that often took three quarters of an hour to complete every day, was Karen, who was four, sitting at the table with me as I worked on my lesson. She'd get a Bible and paper and pencil and tediously copy down what I thought were random letters. One day I asked her what she was doing. "My Bible 'tudy," she said.

Later when I looked at her paper filled with upper and lower case alphabet letters, I was surprised to see a distinct message from Revelation 22:20, "I am coming soon."

In 1976, I wrote my second book, a small book entitled, *What Kids Katch from Parents*, published by Harvest House Publishers. My premise was exactly what Karen was doing. One of the chapters was "Caught, not Taught," and how true it is children do "catch" things from us. Hopefully, for the most part, right and good things!

But Karen wasn't the only one learning. I was reminded again, among other things, about the importance of forgiveness. My inability to forgive my father lay dormant. "Out of sight, out of mind." But as I daily studied God's Word, I became convicted that unless I could forgive my father, my Heavenly Father would not forgive me (Matthew 6:14-15). And when we studied

Paul's letter to the Colossian Church, he, in no uncertain terms, said, "Forgive as the Lord forgave you" (3:13). I knew I had to do something about this deep-seated unwillingness to forgive that was keeping me in a prison.

I began to change my prayer from, "Lord, help me to be willing to forgive my dad," to, "Lord, I do want to forgive my dad. Please help me."

When not faced with a foe, it's easy to forget hatred or a need to forgive. But these two rear their ugly heads when we come face to face with our enemy. Such was the case every time we went up to Canada on our way to Thetis Island for our vacation. I would walk into my parents' home and "wham!" While I was away from the situation, I felt I was beginning to conquer this monster, but it was still there. Nevertheless, on the next visit, I reached out to my dad and gave him a hug. Not much for some, but for me, a victory.

As I came to the end of my five-year BSF study, the last three as a discussion leader, I came to a shocking realization. I had gone to the mission field and come back and only now was I truly understanding some of the in-depth truths of Scripture. How important, as Eugene Peterson in *The Message* paraphrases Colossians 3:15, to: "Let the Word of Christ—the Message—have the run of the house. Give it plenty of room in your lives. Instruct and direct one another using good common sense."

And that's just what I found myself doing. As the Word penetrated my heart, I wanted to share it with others and God opened doors for me to speak at women's retreats, women's groups and lead neighborhood Bible studies.

My first neighborhood Bible Study was at my friend Susan La Flamme's home. We prayed several weeks about this, asking God to lead us to just the right person to lead it. Now that I wasn't involved with BSF, God began to work in my heart that I should lead it. I didn't say anything, but one day after our prayer time, Susan looked at me and said, "I think you should lead it." I smiled and told her God had already been speaking to me about it.

We set the date and time. Susan had flyers made and delivered them to all her neighbors on her street announcing we would begin in two weeks. I struggled to know what we should study. I wanted something elementary for non-Christians, but we would also have a few of our Christian friends who had asked if they could come.

The next week I prayed daily asking God for wisdom as to what we should study. And then one day as I was on my knees praying about this, I heard in my mind "Psalms." Somehow I knew this was right and wrote a series of 12 studies from various Psalms highlighting King David's life.

It was the first and only time I taught a Bible study with a smoking and non-smoking section. But it didn't take long before I knew God had given me the right study and the right words to share.

Gloria was one of the neighbors who came. She burst in and announced, "I'm coming to this study, but you need to know I'm mad at God." She followed this by telling us she had married a widower with two young children after his wife died of cancer. Almost immediately he came down with cancer and she nursed him until he passed away. No sooner had she buried him and been left with two teenage stepchildren than she was diagnosed with cancer.

Gloria didn't miss a week, and wanted to know what we were going to study after the Psalms. In my private devotions I had been reading in 1 John and was struck with verse 6: "Whoever claims to live in Him must walk as Jesus did." I decided to discover just how Jesus walked on earth and zero in on His attitude toward others in various situations.

About the second week of our study, Gloria announced she had a poem she would like to read. She began, "Now that I've found Him, now that I belong, my whole attitude has been so wrong..." She had never written poetry before and was as amazed as the rest of us that she had written in rhyme how she had come to faith. She went on to write some sixty poems before the Lord took her home a few months after she could no longer come to the study.

During this time, I began to struggle over the leadership role of women in the church. I was being asked to speak to mixed Sunday School classes but had been brought up "closed" Plymouth Brethren where, if men were present, women didn't pray out loud. And, of course, women never took a leadership role in meetings. They took seriously the verse in 1 Corinthians 14:34, "....women should remain silent in the churches."

I had learned to pray out loud in Mexico and felt comfortable praying in front of men, but I wasn't sure I should teach if men were present. I read many books like *Daughters of the Church,* by Ruth A. Tucker and Walter Liefeld, *Women at the Crossroads*, by Kari Torjesen Malcom, *I Suffer Not a Woman* by Richard Clark Kroeger and Catherine Clark Kroeger, and *Equal to Serve* by Gretchen Gaebelein Hull, but Paul's verses in 1 Corinthians and 1

Timothy 2:11-15 were my waterloo. After careful study, however, I did have peace that Paul's words regarding women in the early church were cultural because other passages clearly indicated women were in leadership in the early church. But I still was saying "No" when asked.

One day, as I was sitting in an orthodontist's waiting room while Karen was getting braces, I was reading in one of the above books, and came to a statement that made sense to me. The writer pointed out that what was in focus was *obedience*. Were we saying "no" to what God had planned for us? Were there areas in our lives where we were directing our own steps? I stopped and began to pray silently asking God if there were areas where I was stubbornly refusing to do what He wanted me to do. I wanted to know. It's then I heard that soft inner voice say, "What about speaking my messages?" Right there in the waiting room, the tears began to flow, and I knew the next time I was asked to give a Bible study to a mixed group, I would do it.

I continued to lead Bible studies in homes and began to speak to mixed Sunday School classes until 1990. That's when Kristi, our daughter-in-law asked me to lead a Bible study at our church for young mothers. We called the study "Women of the Word" or "WOW." I learned in that study to talk over crying babies as several young mothers brought their newborns with them.

It was a wonderful couple of years. I would have continued but my father was still living on his own at almost 90 and in need of additional care. We returned to Canada for two years to help him and to work half time at Granville Chapel in Pastoral Care. I will pick up the story again from those years in Canada, but I need to go back and share a little of what happened in the children's lives in the intervening years.

Karen always had an interest in music. As a baby she would rock in time to music and when she was around four or five she would get a snorkel and pretend it was a flute. The following year a young woman from Mexico visited us on her way to Biola University and let Karen play on her flute. She was hooked and she wanted the real thing! However, she had to wait until she was in the third grade before joining the band. We were able to get her a nickel student flute that she played throughout her elementary and intermediate school years.

We still didn't feel we could afford private lessons but she was exhibiting great talent in her Jr. High band and her band teacher, Mr. Lester, offered to give her a few private lessons at no charge. Years later, Wendy met Mr. Lester when he came to their church in northern California and she was able to tell him how Karen went on to study at Chapman College (now University) and was a professional flutist. We were always grateful for Mr. Lester reaching out and giving Karen a head start.

In 1981, Karen was fourteen and won an opportunity to play in Crystal Cathedral's Mother's Day program along with her 16-year-old friend, Sharon Chang, a pianist. Out of 150 musicians, they were two of fourteen that were chosen. The program was televised and they played *Sonatina* by Clemente flawlessly.

Karen began flute lessons when she was thirteen with Linda White, on staff at Trinity Presbyterian Church's Music Department, for $7.00 a week until her junior year in high school. That's when we switched to Arthur

. . . .

Hoberman, a college-level teacher at Chapman College, and the cost for weekly flute lessons jumped to $35.00. But we were in for even a larger strain on our missionary budget.

She had won competitions with her nickel flute but would always be told, "You need a better flute!" Finally, when Hugh was on one of his trips, he was able to get a silver semi-professional model in Singapore for $800.00 and eventually in college, Mr. Hoberman found her a used professional Powell flute that cost $5000.00.

I remember going over with the check to Chapman College as I wanted to make sure she really needed this flute. Mr. Hoberman assured me she did. I said, "This is like giving you my left arm. This money is our income tax rebate and was supposed to be for a new roof on our house!" He just smiled. He was right, of course. She could not have gone on without a better flute that enabled her to graduate summa cum laude in Music Performance from Chapman College. (I should mention that about three years later we were able to put on a roof, thanks to son David who gave us a generous gift.)

After graduation, Karen gave flute lessons and had her own studio for a while. She performed in many venues, but in 1993 she knew, if she was ever to get out on her own, she needed to earn more money. She enrolled in the University of California at Irvine, earned her California Teacher's Certificate and taught elementary grades in Irvine and Orange. She also led children's choirs and bell choirs at Trinity and has stated many times how privileged she was to have had all those years under the direction of Trinity's Minister of Worship and Music, Dr. Hanan Yaqub.

. . . .

She married Chris Romig on August 10, 1996 at Trinity with Rev. George Munzing officiating. It was another lovely Steven family wedding with all her siblings taking part, including nieces and nephews.

Chris still needed another year at Princeton Theological Seminary to get his M.Div., so while Chris studied, Karen taught school, and then they received a call to Trinity Presbyterian Church in Satellite Beach, Florida where Chris was Associate Pastor. After six years Chris became senior pastor at Venice Presbyterian Church in Venice, Florida in 2003. They have two boys, William and Nicholas.

Venice has been a good location for Karen to continue her love of music. She not only plays for church services, but Chris, an accomplished pianist, and Karen give concerts in various places. She also plays in the Venice Symphony Orchestra, so while we bemoan they are far away from us, we are grateful she has these wonderful opportunities to use her musical talents. Chris and Karen have released a CD of music entitled, "Music From Around the World."

Chris, Karen, William
Nicholas (in front), 2009

As for Wendy, after college she had lived at home for a while, but then she moved out on her own with Susan Grace (later married to Rev. Gary Watkins) while she taught third grade at Whittier Christian School. She then decided to do something different and for a while worked for Wycliffe Associates while teaching adults English as a Second Language twice a week.

Then on October 9, 1980 we rushed Wendy to Emergency as she was having trouble breathing. She actually had been having breathing difficulties for a few days, but we weren't sure what was going on.

It all began when she had a cyst removed from the side of her nose near her eye. The dermatologist put her on Tetracycline for three weeks prior to the operation and doubled the dose afterwards. When she broke out in a rash and had tightness in her chest, Hugh picked her up from her apartment and brought her home Saturday morning. And when her fever shot up to 104 degrees, we took her to another doctor (her own General Practitioner was not on call that weekend). He thought perhaps it was bronchitis or mononucleosis, gave her a penicillin shot and told us to call him Monday.

Fever, chills and breathing difficulties continued all through Saturday night. I stayed home with her Sunday morning and by 10:00 a.m. felt I should get her to the hospital about a mile from our home.

When Hugh got home from church, he joined me in the Intensive Care waiting room and at 7:00 p.m., Dr. Randazzo, a pulmonary specialist who just "happened" to be in Emergency that weekend, came out and said, "It looks like Legionnaires Disease complicated by double pneumonia. She's very grave. If you are religious people, I suggest you had better start praying."

I think I went into shock, but we got home and called several of our friends who in turn called others and later that evening many stopped by our home to pray with us. At 11:00 p.m. we were all praying when the doctor called us to come to the hospital. Wendy was failing and there was nothing more he could do. Not believing what was happening, yet strengthened by our friends and God's sustaining power, we left with our pastor and his wife, George and Carol Munzing, plus our dear longtime Wycliffe friends, Ben and Adelle Elson, and our son, Dave. Dave's wife Kristi, and our friends Sylvia Chang and Anne Barrett, stayed to be with Karen who was asleep.

How can I explain our anguish? Our lovely Wendy was in the Intensive Care Unit, face swollen, eyes distended and on a respirator with seven tubes protruding from her body. At one point Dr. Randazzo came out to the ICU waiting room, slumped into a chair and said, "I've done all I can do and I'm losing this beautiful girl." We found ourselves comforting him. She finally stabilized at 1:30 a.m. and Dr. Randazzo told us to go home and get some sleep.

But I couldn't sleep. I got up and went into the living room and began to beg God for Wendy's life. I wept and prayed and prayed and wept. At about 4:00 a.m., Hugh came in and put an afghan over my shoulders. I thought he would tell me to come to bed, but he knew I was in anguish. I just couldn't let go and give her up to God. But as I prayed, my tension lessened and I was finally able to say, "Okay, Lord, whatever is Your will. She's yours." And I was able to go to bed and sleep.

. . . .

Over the week she was in Intensive Care, Dr. Randazzo called in nine other specialists. We stayed close by as one diagnosis after another was made, only to be changed the next day. Friends came and went, stopping to pray with us. One dear friend brought us orange juice, a gift we have passed on to others going through the trauma of waiting in ICU while their loved one is clinging to life. We didn't feel like eating, but the orange juice revived us and our spirits.

Then one day, as we sat in the waiting room, we heard the clatter of determined footsteps coming down the hall toward us. In a few moments, my friend and the then Bible Study Fellowship Teaching Leader, Betty Matthews, with about ten discussion leaders in tow, put her head in the door and said, "We've come to pray." And did they pray! I joked later that the ceiling virtually lifted off the rafters! We were so blessed by the love and concern of these women.

Another friend, Doris Grace (her daughter had been Wendy's roommate before she married), was away at the time and heard about Wendy's plight. She called and told us a small church she was attending while there had held a special prayer meeting for Wendy and they all felt she would indeed come through this and get better. I told her I would go on her and their faith as right then I wasn't too sure.

But Wendy did get better. Mike Harvey, the son-in-law of our Wycliffe friends, Ben & Adelle Elson, was a pharmacist and worked at the hospital where the doctors were still trying to discover the cause of Wendy's problem. On his own time he searched the medical records to see if there were any other cases of an allergic reaction to

. . . .

tetracycline. We had told him this was our theory since Wendy had several allergies to medications in the past, even Vitamin C.

Mike did find three cases where patients had died from allergic reactions to tetracycline, and the mystery was solved. It was also discovered that Wendy was allergic to sulfa and now she wears a bracelet at all times to inform medical personnel of her allergies should she be unable to tell them.

Wendy was in ICU a week. We put out many SOS's for prayer as her fever shot up to 106 degrees at one point and the doctors were still grappling with what she had and what the best medications should be. She was on a respirator and the doctor warned us she needed to start breathing on her own or she would be in danger of suffering brain damage. Hugh actually had to be quite firm with her to get her to try breathing on her own. It was just easier and less painful to let the machine do it for her. Finally she did start to breathe on her own but remained on oxygen for the two weeks she was out of ICU but still in the hospital.

After a month's recuperation with us she was finally well enough to go back to work for Wycliffe Associates. How we thanked God for sparing our dear daughter. I wrote about this in a long newsletter and ended by saying, "Pray that our lives as a family will continue to be lived for His glory." I should have added, "…and the display of His splendor!"

After Wendy was well again, she moved to Canada and worked for a year at Trinity Western University in their Admissions office. It was here she picked up a friendship again with a young pastor in Seattle, Rev. Greg

. . . .

Asimakoupoulos, whom she knew from her college years. But that's her story and perhaps she'll write it one day.

After that year's courtship, the date for their wedding was set for May 29, 1982, but not before David and Kristi presented us with our second grandson, Jonathan Paul, born on May 21 weighing nine pounds, thirteen ounces and 22 ½ inches long. It didn't surprise us that he went on to become a professional basketball player! David and Kristi had another son, Andrew James, born March 18, 1986, and Wendy and Greg later presented us with three granddaughters, Kristin, Allison and Lauren.

A P.S. to Wendy's near-death experience was our interaction with Dr. Randazzo. We bought a Living Bible and had his name inscribed on it in gold. In the flyleaf I thanked him for his excellent care of Wendy, bringing in nine specialists, and I wrote that God had used him to save Wendy's life.

A week later she had an appointment at his office and because she was still weak, I drove her and went into the office with her. Wendy was called in and as I was sitting in the waiting room, out came Dr. Randazzo. He wanted to thank me for the Bible and tell me he and his wife were reading the Bible every night to their children.

In our January 1981 newsletter we wrote:

"Some of the things we learned through Wendy's experience are: the complete trustworthiness of God; more insight into how to comfort; life is a precious gift to cherish each day; gratefulness for the ability to breathe (when Wendy was gasping for breath and there was almost none, it was one of the hardest things I had to watch); our lives are in His capable hands; He gives strength to endure when we feel at the end of ourselves; and that we really do need each other to help bear our burdens."

Wendy, Greg, Lauren, Kristin, Allison, 2007

To catch up on Dave, while at Baylor, in 1974 he had the opportunity to play in the Cotton Bowl. He married his high school sweetheart, Kristi Robbins, and went on to play professional football in the Canadian Football League. His second year he played for the Denver Broncos in the National Football League. Given the physical beating most professional football players receive, it was probably a blessing in disguise he didn't continue to play. But if he's just trying to impress someone, his masculine side has been known to come to the fore with the remark, "I had one NFL pass reception for a first down. How many did you have?" That's our competitive Dave!

He came home to begin his career in mortgage banking and is currently a commercial lender with the Evangelical Christian Credit Union (ECCU) as Vice President of Secondary Markets.

Christmas 2008. Front, L. to R.: Luke, Jonathan, Andrew
Back: Heather, David Jr., Kristi, Dave

While a member of Trinity, he took a two-year Bethel Bible Course at Trinity and continues to teach Bible studies for his adult Sunday School class at Richfield Community Church where He and Kristi are active members.   Kristi is on the Worship Team and Dave has been involved in several mission trips to Mexico to help build houses. They are both enjoying being grandparents to Luke David (our first great grandson), son of their oldest son David Jr. and Heather (nee Sielaff). David Jr. is Director of Information Services at Broadview Mortgage.   Their middle son Jonathan played professional basketball for several years and is seeking new direction at this writing, and Andrew, is a worship leader and graphic artist.

Lee, at age 15, left on July 1, 1977 to spend two weeks at Teen Mission's boot camp in Florida. This was his own decision after reading about it in *Campus Life*, a Christian teen magazine. He then moved on to Merida, Yucatan, Mexico with 25 other teens and four leaders to help build a new school designed to minister to children with Down syndrome.

Lee was accepted at Wheaton College and began in the fall of 1980. In April 1983, he went for a two-week mission trip to Honduras with several other Wheaton students to help rebuild homes destroyed by floods the previous year. It was a time of testing when two-thirds of the group came down sick the first week they were there. Commenting on this experience, Lee wrote: "Each one of us is seeing life just a bit differently than we did before and I think we are seeing God more clearly. We are realizing more and more that we are totally inadequate in ourselves, and that we have to turn to God for all our strength."

Between his junior and senior year Lee spent seven months in Papua New Guinea with a development group, the Lutheran Economic Service, to build a waterwheel in a remote village to provide electricity for a literacy house where people were learning to read and write in their own language. This was part of the Human Needs and Global Resources (HNGR) program that he participated in while at Wheaton. During his time in PNG, he visited a Wycliffe missionary and in a letter dated January 24, 1984, he wrote: "I hiked six hours into the village and let me tell you, it was one of the hardest hikes I have ever made! There wasn't 100 yards of flat ground the whole way and the mountain paths went straight up and down. Talk about virgin jungle, this place was it. Everywhere the place was crawling with leeches. By the time I got to the village, I must have pulled well over 50 leeches off my legs."

L. to R.: Marshall, Isabel, Walker, Paula, Lee, July 2009

Lee graduated from Wheaton College in 1985 with a B.S. in Chemistry, earning high honors. A week later, on May 11, 1985, he married Paula Ditzler (whom he met at Wheaton) in her parents' beautiful apple orchard near Rosedale, Indiana. Almost thirty years to the day after we took our field training (then called "Jungle Camp"), Lee and Paula were taking their field training for service with Wycliffe Bible Translators, this time in Uvalde, Texas. They also spent a month in Mexico living with a Mexican family, but they had many of the same experiences we did, such as, killing chickens, building furniture, making a mud stove, hikes, etc.

They were assigned to the Island of Roma in Indonesia and made excellent headway in the language. In 1990, however, the government was not renewing visas, and since Paula was pregnant with their first child, they came home to Wycliffe's linguistic training headquarters in Dallas, Texas where Lee completed his MA. in linguistics and taught new Wycliffe recruits linguistics, phonology and field methods.

Lee and Paula spent four years in Dallas where they had two children, Walker and Isabel. They subsequently resigned from Wycliffe and moved to Charlottesville, Virginia where their third child, Marshall, was born. In Charlottesville, Lee studied law at the University of Virginia. After graduation from law school he began work with the law firm of White & Case in Washington, D.C. They currently live in Fredericksburg, Virginia.

I've skimmed over the children's accomplishments, but in the following chapters I'll give a give a few more details and comment on all the books Hugh was writing (and I was typing) during this time.

12

Books, First Grandchild, Last Birthday

All these years the children were growing up, going off to college, getting married and starting their own families, Hugh was writing books, and at last count he's written 32, ghosted several others and we've both edited books for many other authors—Hugh says about 50!

In those early days before computers, if there were additions or changes to be made in Hugh's manuscript, I would sometimes have to type his books three or four times. I did most of my typing in a corner of our dining room on a Selectric typewriter (at least it was better than the manual typewriters I used in Mexico). But it was tedious work. After a few years of this and seeing no end in sight, when I turned 50, after a particularly busy Christmas season when I was also working part-time in a Christian bookstore to help with finances, I went into a downward spiral. The thought of spending another twenty years staring at my dining room wall while sitting at the typewriter sent me into a deep depression for about six weeks. Eventually I came out of it through praying often nothing more than "help!" I've never been sorry for that experience even though during those weeks displaying God's splendor in my life was distant. As Miss Johnson from BSF says, "Nothing is wasted with God." It has helped me to understand and be more sympathetic to others in similar situations.

By January 1972, we were praising God for the good reception Hugh's second book, *You Eat Bananas* was having. It came out in 1971 and had a second printing the same year. And now he had two more books coming out in February and April. They were *Miracles in Mexico*, co-authored with Jim Hefley, and *Night of the Long Knives and Other Adventure Stories* that went on to earn the distinction of being one of ten top children's books for the year for the Evangelical Christian Schools. Hugh had a non-Wycliffe book come out in 1972 as well. It was *The Reproducers*, the story of the beginnings of Chuck Smith's ministry and the expansion of the first Calvary Chapel in Costa Mesa, California.

In addition, Hugh published twenty articles, had a five-week trip to Columbia, Panama and Mexico and while in Mexico, attended the Otomi New Testament dedication. We remembered when we first went out to the Otomi area in the years 1958-63 and had taken out the first copies of Acts. After reading a few verses, our Otomi Indian friend Raul said, "How beautiful!" and now they had the whole New Testament.

In 1972, Hugh's passport was also clearly marked with, "Republic of Viet Nam, Philippines, and Territory of Papua New Guinea." The purpose of this trip, like his other trips, was to bring back photos and information that would highlight how God was working through the translated Scriptures.

Hugh also had the opportunity of working again with Cornell Capa, "Life" photographer, who was instrumental in beginning his journey into journalism when he traveled with him in 1966 for the dedication of the Tzeltal New Testament. This time Hugh worked with him and other Wycliffe personnel on a new Wycliffe pictorial volume entitled, *Language and Faith.*

While Hugh was writing new books, we rejoiced that his first book, *Manuel* had, by 1974, come out in British, French and German editions while Finnish, Dutch and Spanish editions were in the works. We noted in an April 15th newsletter that Wycliffe had moved its international headquarters from Santa Ana to a "lovely spacious office building in Huntington Beach, California" and that Wycliffe now had 3100 members from 22 countries working in 28 fields.

In 1974, Hugh had another book published, *It Takes Time to Love,* and I was working on my third book, *Homemaking, an Invitation to Greatness,* that came out in 1978. I co-wrote this with Joyce Orwick, whom I never met. She was a young mother of four and had read my book, *What Kids Katch from Parents* and found it helpful. Now she wanted help in her role as a homemaker. I shared her letters and mine along with housekeeping hints, recipes and thoughts from the Word. I felt because I used her letters, her name should also be on the cover.

If you wonder about the title and why homemaking is an invitation to greatness, just read Matthew 20:26: "Whoever wants to become great among you must be your servant." Who serves more than a homemaker?

In 1975, *Manuel* came out in yet another edition. This time it was Portuguese, and we told our friends and donors to look for Hugh's new book, *Kim.* He had been asked by Harvest House Publishers to do this story on Kim Wickes, a blind Korean singer. It turned out to be a difficult task for Hugh, who had made a trip to Calgary and Mexico gathering material for new books and articles and was working on this material at the same time. He was so stressed, he began to have pain in his liver. One doctor was ready to do a biopsy on his liver, but Hugh got a second opinion and this doctor felt the pain would disappear once he had one of his two book projects off his slate, and it proved to be true.

In April 1976, we began our newsletter with facts and figures. I asked the question, "Did you know that Wycliffe…"

--Began work in 1935?
--Has 8 schools to train translators?
--Is now working in 26 countries in 663 languages?
--Has a membership of 3,497?
--Has members from 26 countries?
--Enters a new language group every 13 days?
--Has published 57 New Testaments?
--Workers take about 15 years to translate a New Testament?
--Knows of 2,000 languages still needing God's Word?

We also noted that on May 5th we celebrated our 25th wedding anniversary, August marked our 20th year as missionaries with Wycliffe, my parents celebrated their 51st wedding anniversary, Lee was named top boy student of his 8th grade graduation class and received a medal, and Lee and Karen publicly declared their decision to follow Jesus as they were baptized in the Pacific Ocean by Pastor Chuck Smith of Calvary Chapel. Wendy and David had been baptized by immersion in 1968 in Buffalo Grove when we attended a new American Baptist church that met in Lee's school. They, along with another child, were the first to be baptized by the young pastor. We had to go into Chicago to use another church's baptismal.

Manuel, was continuing to get good mileage. It went into a third printing and a second printing in German. *Night of the Long Knives* was now out in a Dutch edition and *The Measure of Greatness,* published in 1973, and *It Takes Time to Love* went into second printings.

In September 1976, Hugh had a five-week trip to Mexico, Suriname, Brazil and Peru. In a newsletter we asked for "wisdom, insight and sensitivity as he writes articles from the material he gathered, and a book on what God is doing through Bible translation in Brazil." Hugh's book, *They Dared to be Different* on Ken Jacobs work amongst the Chamulas in Southern Mexico, was also published.

In a June 20, 1977 newsletter we announced Dave & Kristi's engagement along with Dave's disappointment at not making the Winnipeg Blue Bombers football team. Then in our December 19th letter, we told our readers that one person had said it was a "jewel of a wedding." And indeed it was. And to top it off, my mother came for a three-week visit, her first trip to California.

There was only one thing Mama wanted to do, other than attend Dave & Kristi's wedding, and that was to go to Disneyland and see Mickey and Minnie Mouse. In the midst of all the excitement of the wedding, we did find time to go, and whom do you think we met when we walked in the entrance? Right! Mickey and Minnie, and Mama went right up to them, hugged them, and I snapped a picture. Mama cherished that photo and we also put it on a T-shirt for Karen. She wore and wore that T-shirt, and as far as I know, she still has it stored away as a keepsake!

November 1978 brought the happy news that we would be grandparents for the first time in February. Wendy had a good summer at Forest Home Family Conference Center where she counseled high school kids and taught five and six-year-olds and was now teaching thirty third graders at Whittier Christian School. Karen was playing flute in a marching band and taking piano lessons from Kristi. Hugh had a trip to Ecuador to gather story material, and his book, *To the Ends of the Earth*, on Wycliffe's work in Brazil, had come out in May.

Saturday, February 24, 1979, our first grandchild was born. It was as exciting as if it had been our own. Hugh wrote:

"It's a boy!" said Lee. I was outside sawing up the old plum tree. I stood up, chuckled, and repeated to myself, "A boy; a child; a grandchild. Our first grandchild. How incredible! Praise God for His great gifts!" He's nine pounds (another football player?), 21 inches, and Kristi and Dave, the oh-so-very-proud parents, named him David Craig Jr.

Indeed it was incredible, and as I saw David Craig Jr. for the first time, I was speechless. Only later did I pick up my pencil and write out my thoughts in rhyme:

As I look into his little face,
There's something there of me.
Is it his eyes, his nose his mouth?

What is it that I see?
It's there, though blurred, and twice removed,
A faint image of me.
As God looks down upon my life,
What image does He see?
His child am I though faith in Christ,
He's living now in me.
Do I portray His likeness? Or is it slightly blurred--
More grandchild than His faithful child,
A light in a dark world?

Help me, O Lord, to live my life,
Not grandchild, but as child,
That others looking on will say,
"She's God's and undefiled;
Her life she lives in kindness,
She's walking free of sin,
Her faith's so bright, we all can see
A clear image of Him."

Everything else seemed anticlimactic after this new little one came into our lives, but that year Moody Press published Hugh's book, *The Man with the Noisy Heart*, the story about Wycliffe's chief translation coordinator, John Beekman. And if that wasn't enough to celebrate, *Danger in the Blue Lagoon*, Hugh's children's book, was also published. It was quite a year. Hugh would have finished his book on Ecuador but was momentarily sidetracked by an assignment to be the associate producer for a new Wycliffe recruitment film. This entailed a two-week trip to the Philippines to get the film ready for Urbana, Inter-Varsity's large missions conference between Christmas and New Year's. Wendy and Lee attended the Urbana Conference that year enabled by Trinity giving them full scholarships. Lee was also looking into what university he should attend in the following year. Karen continued to pursue her musical studies adding piccolo and saxophone to her flute and piano. Wendy was now working for Wycliffe Associates and working weekends as an Aide Coordinator at Forest Home Christian Camp and Conference Center where Lee also spent a five-week leadership training camp in the summer.

While all this was going on, I was kept busy editing and typing Hugh's books and also writing Bible studies I hoped to get published. One study I called, *Lord, I'm Right Behind You,* a series of nine Bible studies. I also wrote an allegory, *Consider the Seed,* but that along with many, many Bible studies are still tucked away in my filing cabinet. I used all the Bible studies in my teaching, but none were ever published.

Nineteen eighty was a year filled with challenges, sadness and gladness. The challenges came when our kitchen cupboards were refinished and in a newsletter I wrote: "If you've never stripped cupboards, re-stained and varnished them--don't! But they do look beautiful and we almost think it was worth all the labor." Hugh had the challenge of giving a creative communication seminar at Northwest Baptist Theological College in Vancouver, B.C., Canada and a weeklong writers' workshop at Regent College, also in Vancouver.

The sadness was that just two weeks before Christmas my mother had a massive stroke affecting her right side. I will never forget calling her and trying to understand her slurred speech. When she tried to tell me she loved me, I just sobbed. I went up for two weeks in January and my dad actually expressed gratefulness for my coming. He was at the point of collapse trying to look after Mama. I went back for a week in March as well.

The gladness was Hugh's book *Manuel* that came out in a Danish edition bringing the total number of editions to eight. And *The Man with the Noisy Heart* went into a second printing. His book about Wycliffe's work in Ecuador, *Never Touch a Tiger* came out in the summer and in September Hugh traveled to Pt. Barrow, Alaska with Wycliffe translator Don Webster to research translation work among the Inupiats for a book he would title, *Good Broth to Warm our Bones*.

With Hugh being gone so much and leaving me with the children and all their day-to-day problems, an interesting unhealthy attitude began to creep into my psyche. I found myself becoming resentful. Gone were the lofty thoughts about living my life for "the display of His splendor." All that was in my mind was why did he get all the fun? Why did I have to stay home when other missionary wives went on trips with their husbands? Why couldn't I go?

I fretted about that for some time until I finally got to go on a trip with Hugh to take part in writers' workshops in Alaska in 1984, and Australia and Vanuatu in 1987. I began to see it wasn't all "sweetness and light." I guess in my mind's eye I was thinking nice hotel rooms and good food. I found out flying twenty-one hours non-stop in a hot plane, time changes, extreme heat, strange accommodations, uncomfortable transportation and unpredictable food could hardly be described as a vacation trip. But then these trips were not designed as vacations.

They were working trips, so what did I expect? I knew Hugh, in his many travels, had slept on primitive, unprotected airstrips when the plane couldn't get in to fly him out, and on other occasions in tumble down, noisy hotels, and longhouses with many other people, but he assured me it wouldn't be like that on these trips. And it wasn't. But after a couple of tiring trips, there was no more resentment, no more complaining. I was happy to stay at home while Hugh went off on his assignments!

Hugh's books continued to have a wide circulation. There were British and Philippine editions plus a sixth printing in English with a German edition going into a second printing. *They Dared to be Different* was out in German with *Miracles in Mexico* coming out in a Swedish edition and *Night of the Long Knives* in Dutch and German editions.

In our July 1982 newsletter, we had more sad news about my mother. She had been diagnosed with lung cancer even though she and my dad had never smoked. She had wanted to come for Wendy and Greg's wedding and even bought a dress, but Dad said if she came, she didn't have to bother coming back. After that disappointment she began to rapidly fail.

With Wendy's wedding on the horizon and my mother's health failing, it was soon evident Hugh needed another secretary. I was not keeping up with the work he had for me and with wedding preparations and needing to make a bridesmaid dress for Karen, I was desperate. Enter Valarie Sluss.

Hugh had met her in Huntington Beach where she had been working for four years in the Publications office of

Wycliffe's U.S. headquarters. She later quit and when Hugh heard she was looking for work, he contacted her. I was so grateful, as she was an excellent typist, able to do some editing, and she was willing to do the tedious job of transcribing interview tapes.

With her Wycliffe background, Val's help was invaluable. She married Robert Stevenson four years later and moved to Hawaii, but when they returned, Hugh would send her tapes to transcribe and manuscripts to type right up until a few years ago.

We did have secretarial help for two years in the late 70s when Jocelyn and Wayne Cameron came from Calgary, Alberta, Canada and bought a house a few blocks from us. Hugh had met the Camerons and stayed with them when he was on the board of Wycliffe Canada. While Jocelyn helped Hugh and eased my workload, Wayne worked with Wycliffe Associates. It was a sad day when they left!

We had one last family celebration with twenty family members for Mama's 80th birthday on July 20. I wondered what to give her for her birthday as we all knew the end was near. I prayed about it and thought I'd give her something she liked very much—opening gifts!

I am a little box saver. Hugh asked me for years what I was going to do with them all. I never knew, but now I did. I picked out fourteen, enough for one a day for two weeks before her birthday. Inside I put decorated half sheets of 8 ½ x 11 sheets with what I called gifts Mama had given me over the years by what she had either taught or demonstrated in her life. Gifts like self-denial, friendship, acceptance, Godliness, joy, love, generosity, sense of humor, compassion, sensitivity, faithfulness, motherhood, dignity and hard work.

On the paper entitled "Dignity" I wrote:

Dignity, or self-worth is a precious gift you have given me. Because you love me, I know I have value. I didn't need to find out who I was or what I was worth by getting into the wrong crowd or being rebellious. Because you gave me a sense of dignity, I wanted to live up to your expectations. This has always helped me to remember I'm a child of the King, too. I never wanted to cause you pain or embarrassment and I don't want to cause my heavenly Father sadness either. You have made me feel dignified—like royalty—because this is how you are. You are a beautiful woman and I'm proud to be your daughter.

Under "Hard Work" I wrote:

From the time we worked together in the strawberry and raspberry fields when I was 13 until now, you have shown me that hard work never hurt anyone. I have never wanted to be lazy or slothful because you never were. And because you weren't afraid to tackle what came your way, I've also tried to do the same thing—be it wall papering, painting or gardening.

You've also challenged me to try new things by your example of learning to type when you were in your sixties. You have worked hard all your life and shown me how. Thank you, for this is a helpful, special gift.

For "Faithfulness" I wrote:

When I think of your faithfulness to Dad and to God, I am most grateful. Your example is hard to find in today's world. You committed your life to Dad for better or worse, in sickness and in health, in plenty and in want, for as long as you live, and you've been faithful to that vow. Your stick-to-itiveness has been a shining example to me of not looking for a way out when things are rough. In the same way, your faithful walk with God has been a great gift to me. There are many times in life when God seems far away and we want to question, "Why God? Why me?" Yet your faithful walk with Him brings back God's words time and time again when I'm tempted to doubt: "What is that to thee, follow thou me." Thank you for staying true to your marriage vows and commitment to Christ.

I loved my mother's laughter. I knew I wanted to thank her for her sense of humor:

If I try, I can hear your laughter whenever I want! It's there, ringing in my ears. You have to be the cutest 80-year-old I've ever known! You love a good joke and can sure make your own! Thank you for your gift of a good sense of humor. I think one of the funniest things you ever said was in the Hippie heyday. You couldn't

. . . .

understand why everyone was upset with them. "They can't be that bad," you said. "After all, they like flowers!" You taught me how to laugh at myself and not take things too seriously. I can laugh even now when I think of you trying to get away with those strange Scrabble words. And as for playing Scrabble by yourself with Dad as an imaginary foe and you always managing to win, I smile just thinking about it. You have shown me how to enjoy life even in the simplest things. Thank you!

Mama was one of the most compassionate people I knew, so I had to thank her for living her life with compassion when she could have become hardened by her testings and trials in her life with Dad.

Thank you for giving me the gift of compassion. Our children know you love and care for them by your get-well cards, letters and telephone calls. I remember when I stayed with you after my hemorrhoidectomy. I was groaning in the bathroom and you stood outside the door and said, "Oh, I'm so sorry. I'd gladly bear your pain if I could." You looked after me through childhood diseases and on into adulthood when I've been ill. Remember those six weeks I had with you when I came up from Mexico? I was pregnant with Karen and had just had hepatitis and para-typhoid the year previously and I was quite ill. You nursed me back to health by allowing me to just rest and relax while you pampered me with your good cooking. And you enjoyed getting to know four-year-old Lee! Thank you for your gift of compassion that has taught me how to care.

There was one gift I couldn't leave out that left a lasting impression on me. It was "joy."

You had joy even when your heart was breaking and troubles crushed you. Through childhood and when I've visited you over the years, your joy has spilled out in song. I remember you singing while doing the laundry, singing while washing a floor, singing first thing while making breakfast. You have shown me how to "rejoice always," no matter what. Somehow your singing always reassures me that everything is okay. It's a wonderful gift. You just make people feel good! Thank you for your gift of joy.

All the "gifts" I put in the little boxes are worth sharing, but just one more. She was such a good mother I felt I needed to comment on her gift of motherhood she gave me through her example, so I wrote:

How many school and church programs did you sit through? Because you were always there, you taught me the importance of doing the same for my children. What an example of a good mother you've been! This gift really is a collection of all the other gifts you've given me. Your love, compassion, non-judgmental, generous, sensitive godly ways have given me a great example of what a mother should be. Thank you for who you are. "Mother" is a very precious word to me because of you.

I wrapped each of the fourteen boxes in different wrapping paper and different ribbons and put them all in another larger box I wrapped in colorful paper and tied with a big bow. I wrapped the lid separately so she could take if off easily every day for two weeks. However, after she opened the first one she coyly asked if she could open another and then another. She was having such fun I hated to stop her, but we were leaving for a week at Thetis and coming back to celebrate her birthday and I wanted her to have something to open while we were gone. After she had opened six of them I told her to wait until we were gone to open the others. My idea was for her to open them one a day, but I have a sneaking suspicion she probably opened them all when we left.

The birthday party was a success, we went back to southern California and I came up again in September for three weeks. November 1st we received a call that Mama was in the hospital and fading. I was able to get up to Canada again on November 5th and five   days later she was ushered into heaven but not before God dealt with me once more about my need to forgive my dad.

13

Forgiveness, Coronation, Alaska

My younger sister Shirley arrived from Victoria to be with Mom for the last few days of her life. Dad was bringing her mid-morning and would bring us both back in the evening. But by about the third day, he decided he wasn't going to drive her to the hospital that day. I was so annoyed I thought I was just not going to make him coffee that evening like I had been doing. He didn't deserve it.

While the nurses attended to my mother, I went out to the waiting room and picked up my book on the Beatitudes by Lloyd Ogilvie. "Blessed are the merciful," I read, "for they shall obtain mercy." Rev. Ogilvie wrote about God's great mercy toward us and how we should not withhold mercy from others. I began to squirm. It was as if the Lord said to me, "After all the mercy I've shown you, after all I've forgiven you, you can't forgive your father one more time or show him mercy?"

I knew what I would have to do. That night as he drove me home, I decided to go in to make his coffee. As I willingly did what I felt God wanted me to do, this simple act of making coffee took on an amazingly new dimension.

. . . .

It wasn't just a case of showing mercy to my father. In obedience, I was making coffee for the Lord and as such, it was an act of worship. I actually had joy in what I was doing and had progressed to the place, after almost thirty years, where I wanted to forgive my father and forget. No, I didn't say, "I forgive you, Dad." In my heart I knew I did, but I also knew if I said such a thing to him, he would lash out at me never thinking for a moment he had done anything for which I needed to forgive him. I also wasn't sure if, after an absence and I saw him again, the old feelings wouldn't come back. So now it was back to my knees to ask again for God's help. And as I did, I began to see clearer what forgiveness is all about.

"Part of our problem with forgiveness," writes Lewis Smedes in his book "Forgive and Forget," "is realizing that the person who hurt us did not have to. And for that reason we are always left with the mystery of why they did!" But mystery or not, I knew that unless I did forgive my father, I was going to be kept in a wretched prison, and I wanted to get out for good.

Actually, as Christians, we don't have an option. If we don't forgive others, God won't forgive us. And there's the bitterness that envelops us as we replay hurtful memories. If not removed, with each passing year, the bitterness consumes us more and more. I'd seen that happen with my father's interpersonal relationships and I didn't want to end up like him.

The writer of Hebrews tells us in 12:14-15 (italics added): "*Make every effort* to live in peace with all men [and women] and to be holy because without holiness no one will see the Lord. See to it that no one misses the grace of

God and that no *bitter root* grows up to cause trouble and defile many."

About that time I also read a small piece about Clara Barton, the founder of the American Red Cross. One day someone reminded her of a vicious deed that someone had done to her years before. She acted as if she had never heard of the incident.

"Don't you remember it?" said her friend.

"No," came Clara's reply. "I distinctly remember forgetting it."

Clara understood she was an amateur forgiver, that she would have to forgive again and again, but she made "every effort" not to let that "bitter root" grow.

I began to realize it was okay for me to be an amateur forgiver, too. God never intended me to be a professional one. That's why He told Peter that forgiveness is never-ending. We're to forgive seventy times seven—just keep on forgiving over and over again because it isn't a once-for-all exercise. It's an ongoing process.

This was very freeing. Good thing, too, because in ten years I'd be battling with forgiveness again, but right now I was just happy I had been merciful and forgiving to my father that day knowing I had pleased my Heavenly Father.

I walked up the hill to the neighbors where I was staying. I went in and shared with the elderly couple from Mom's church about my day and how hard it was to see my mother suffer.

"I want to share with you a dream I had last night," said the woman. "There was this house with two boards missing on one side and your mother seemed upset. But then I heard a voice say, 'It's all right, Hilda. Just two

. . . .

more boards and we'll be all done.'" Mama died two days later.

I had stayed with her all night and through the night I read underlined portions from her Bible and sang her favorite hymns. She was agitated and kept pulling the oxygen tube out of her nose. I'd put it back in and then sing one of her favorite hymns like *"Lily of the Valley"* and one she particularly liked, *"It Will be Worth it All When We See Jesus."* The rest of that first verse is: *"Our trials seem so small when we see Christ. One glimpse of His dear face, all sorrows will erase, so quickly run the race, 'til we see Christ."* The nurse put her on morphine and she calmed down. I slept a couple of hours in a chair. She was delirious but towards morning she distinctly said, "The Lord is my Helper. I love you all. Lord Jesus, take me home."

At 5:00 a.m., I reminded the nurses that my mother had asked that there be no heroics. They sent me out of the room and I called Shirley to come. She arrived and we went in to Mom's room. Gone were the tubes, the blankets were neatly tucked around her and she was breathing slowly.

The date was November 10, 1982. We stood beside her as she breathed her last and then a beautiful thing happened. We knew she had caught a glimpse of Jesus and He had erased all her sorrows because all the wrinkles in her face disappeared. She looked serene. She was Home. And my first thought was, *she taught me how to live and now she has taught me how to die.*

Hugh's remarks at her passing capsulated her life for us all when he said:

> All of the qualities of love the Bible speaks about in
> 1 Corinthians 13 were lived out in practical ways in

her daily life and have spoken to me more powerfully than any of the hundreds of sermons I have ever heard on how one is to love.

For Easter break 1983, Karen had a week in Mexicali, Mexico with Trinity's Youth Group holding Vacation Bible School in a small village, helping with crafts, giving her testimony in evening services, singing, and playing her flute. They saw 40 or more come to Christ.

While Karen was in Mexico, Hugh traveled to two Wycliffe home offices in Singapore and Tokyo and then flew to Irian Jaya and Sabah to gather material on translation work in those areas.

Later, in June, Hugh traveled to Quebec, Canada to obtain information on Wycliffe's work among the Eastern Cree people. Our newsletter noted he came back with "100 exposed films." It was hard to believe there were no digital cameras during all of Hugh's photography career!

While not traveling like the rest of the family, I was not idle. I took a ten-week evangelism course that entailed a lot of studying, Scripture memorization and practice in sharing my faith. Afterwards I was on a team that went out by twos and threes to visit people who were visitors to our church and we had many opportunities to share our faith.

On September 22, 1983, Wendy and Greg presented us with our first granddaughter. Kristin Nicole Asimakoupoulos. They were living in Concord, California, east of San Francisco, about seven hours north of us where Greg had accepted a call to be Senior Pastor of Crossroads Covenant Church.

I was able to go up for two weeks to help with the new baby, and I enjoyed every minute of it! It was amazing to think that only three years previously we had almost lost Wendy. One of her doctors, commenting on her delivery, said, "Just think. A few years ago Wendy lay dying and now she has given life."

We felt blessed beyond measure when all four children accepted Christ into their lives at a young age. And when in April 1984, grandson David, age 5, told us he had asked Jesus into his heart, we praised God that we had lived to see another generation chosen by God to belong to Him!

Hugh was happy that two of his books, *Never Touch a Tiger*, and *Night of the Long Knives* were put on cassette tapes called "Talking Books." *They Dared to be Different* was out in a new edition with six additional chapters and his first book, *Manuel*, came out in yet two more editions— Greenlandic and Greek. This made a total of twelve different translations and we rejoiced for the worldwide exposure of this book.

He was now working on *A Thousand Trails* that would be the first of four books on the life and times of William Cameron Townsend (affectionately known as "Uncle Cam"), Wycliffe's founder. My contribution to these projects was editing and typing. I was also getting a couple of lectures ready for a writer's workshop in Kotzebue, Alaska from June 11-15 that I would participate in with Hugh doing the bulk of the lecturing.

In our February 1984 newsletter I commented that the total number of language projects in which Wycliffe was

....

involved at that time was 907.   Other Wycliffe statistics
included:

> --No. of languages still needing Bible translation:
> possibly 3,000
> --No. of people represented by these languages: at
> least 200 million
> --No. of adult Wycliffe workers: 5,048
> --No. of countries represented in Wycliffe: 29—
> about 30% from other countries than the U.S.
> --Current No. of personnel needed: Approximately
> 1,465

Hugh's mother and his Auntie Barry Knowles arrived
from Vancouver, B.C. Canada for a two-week visit in April
1984. The day after their arrival, Hugh and I went out for
a few things from the grocery store, and I fell on a slippery
place on the sidewalk and broke my right arm up near the
shoulder.

With my arm in a sling, it was not easy to cook and
entertain, but we had a trip to see Wendy and the family
for a few days, and that helped. It was an inconvenient
break, but amazingly, something good happened out of it.
The next day after my arm was in a sling, we went in to
tell the store manager about the slippery spot from a
broken spigot in their sprinkling system. We were not
intending to sue but thought they should know in order to
fix it and not be taken to the cleaners by some
unscrupulous customer.

The next day we received a call from an attorney
representing the store. He said the manager felt we were
due some money for "pain and suffering." We weren't

. . . .

going to argue with him and when he asked what kind of work I do, I said, "Oh, I just work at home typing and editing." He perked up and said, "We'll have to get you something for that, too." In the end, the check was for almost $5,000 and we were able to get Karen a newer used car that she needed, and years later, we were able to donate that car to Wycliffe for another missionary needing one. Nevertheless, I don't want to go through that again to get a new car. It was painful!

And imagine this. Wycliffe made available for our use our first computer—a Digital Rainbow 100. I feverishly taught myself word processing in preparation for Hugh's next book. And there was the first hint about trying to get more office space. In our October 1984 newsletter I wrote under the heading, "Office Space Needed," "With one typewriter plus supplies in the dining room, the computer in a bedroom, Hugh's resource material in one part of the garage and his office and library in another part, we are in desperate need of more office space if we are to function efficiently. We need wisdom to know what steps to take to alleviate this problem. Please pray."

Now that I had settled the problem of whether or not I should speak to mixed groups, I was speaking regularly in our adult Sunday School classes at Trinity. I was also beginning to write a few articles of my own and had them accepted for publication. And Hugh's book *Manuel* just kept coming out in different languages bringing the number to fourteen with the addition of Icelandic and Indonesian.

By January 1985, Karen had been accepted at Chapman College to major in music performance and Lee was engaged to Paula Ditzler. This was a happy surprise, and they set their wedding for May 11 in Rosedale, Indiana a week after Lee's graduation (Paula had graduated from Wheaton a year previously). Greg officiated, Dave was a groomsman, Karen was a bridesmaid and played her flute, and we all celebrated Communion together. It was a fairy tale wedding in Paula's parents' apple orchard "cathedral" with the reception on the spacious lawn outside the Ditzler's home.

Not to be outdone, I took part in the first Presbyterian Congress on Renewal in Dallas with Rev. Bob Pietsch, Trinity's Associate Pastor. We held a workshop entitled, "Adopting a Christian Lifestyle in a Needy World."

But our special milestones were not finished. Lee graduated from Wheaton earning a Bachelor of Science in Chemistry with high honors. George Bush was the Commencement speaker and I got to say hello to Barbara Bush. Karen graduated from High school and worked at Disneyland for the summer and another blessing was that Karen, Hugh and I counseled at the Anaheim Billy Graham Crusade. Karen also sang in the choir. It was a bit of heaven to hear the 10,000-voice choir and also sing hymns with the 70,000 who attended the last night. Over 6,000 indicated their desire to follow the Lord that night and over 30,000 made first-time commitments or recommitments overall.

In June we left to hold our writers' workshop in Kotzebue, 25 miles inside the Arctic Circle, a village of 25,000 that is 80% Inupiat. It was my first experience of having light 24 hours a day. We were out visiting Wycliffe missionaries, Wolf and Hildegard Seiler (from Germany) and left their house at 11:00 p.m. Children were still out playing and many people were on the shore watching the ice breakup.

Those who came to the workshop wanted to learn how to write their own stories, history and legends. "We've had a lot written about us by outsiders," commented the director of the NANA Museum of the Arctic, which was part of the NANA Regional Corporation, Inc. that sponsored us. "We want to learn how to make our stories interesting for others to read as well as preserve our Eskimo values and culture."

Some of the subjects we covered were:

- The Creative Attitude
- Developing our Senses
- Observation
- Sensitive Listening
- Blocks to Creativity and how to Overcome them
- Going Beyond Facts
- Emotion
- Drama and Action
- Seeing and Feeling Intensely

It was hard to know if we were giving them what they wanted because we couldn't tell what they were thinking. However, after we completed the first assignment of listing sounds with feelings, we felt we were on the right track. The participants, who included two college students, a local pastor, and a high school teacher, were hesitant to read their assignments that first morning, but they agreed to read each other's. Each demonstrated a great depth of feeling and creativity. For example: "The ping of the blueberries slapping the bottom of the birchbark basket..." and "This hiss of the runners on the squeaky snow..."

It was a stimulating experience for me as I read their pieces filled with emotion, sound, conversation, drama and action. And Wolf Seiler later wrote us to tell us there was a side benefit from the workshop. There was a new interest now among many Inupiats in their New Testament translation. Through the workshop and the interest in our helping them to write and publish, the Inupiats realized that the Seilers were in their community for more than language learning and the translation of the Bible. They now understood that others are interested in them as individuals and anxious to help them find outlets for their creativity.

After arriving back home from our Alaska trip, Hugh immediately began teaching a few classes at another writers' conference held at Biola University. And a few weeks later he gave a ten-week writers' workshop at Trinity. All these trips were for material to go into a commemorative volume coming out in 1984, *Pass the Word—50 years of Wycliffe Bible Translators*. Hugh was the director, photographer, writer and editor for this project and I was listed as an associate editor and writer.

14

Memory Albums, New Offices, Australia

In the Spring of 1985, a swollen left knee and ankle, diagnosed as acute bursitis, confined me to bed for three weeks and I began a project for my eventual eleven grandchildren I called "Nana's Memories." I had kept photo albums since before we were married and had numerous photos with captions as well as photos from our parents after they passed away. I began to wonder what I was going to do with them all. I decided with five grandchildren and more to come, I'd divide the photos, keeping some back for future albums, and also use the albums to keep mementoes such as cards, letters, drawings or other keepsakes the grandchildren might send us over the years. So with photo albums covering my bed, I began. It kept me busy for three weeks and at the end of that time, my bursitis was gone!

David, Jonathan, Kristin, Allison, Andrew, Lauren and Walker now have five or six 100-page albums each (the large magnetic-pages for a three-ring binder). When they graduated from high school, I gave the albums to each of them as graduation gifts. The albums contain not only old photos but also current photos they've sent us and photos I've taken when we've been with them. I've included other photos of the extended family as well and given them some history and running commentary for a pictorial history. It's been a labor of love these past twenty-seven years but now that I'm getting older I have to admit I'm glad to be down to just four albums to work on for Isabel, Marshall, William and Nicholas.

While I was confined to bed and working on the photo albums, Hugh was working in his hot office in our unfinished garage as he had been for the past sixteen years. We didn't have air conditioning and the house, as well as Hugh's office, was unbearable in the heat waves during the summer and sometimes at other odd times during the year when the temperatures soared into triple digits. At times the house would be so hot at night it was difficult to sleep and Hugh would try to catch a breeze by sleeping outside on the patio. However, getting air conditioning on our missionary budget was out of the question.

Hugh was able to make a trip to Manuel Arenas's Bible school for the graduation of eight students. "As the Totonac students walked down the aisle to receive their diplomas with Manuel walking behind them," wrote Hugh in our newsletter, "the 200 people who had gathered in the church sang, *Onward Christian Soldiers*. It was a moving experience to witness the results of Bible translation rippling out into other lives."

Hugh's mother was continuing her battle with cancer and was almost completely bedridden. We had been going up summers to Peachland, B.C., Canada to relieve Hugh's brother, Jim, with whom she lived, so he could get away for a vacation.

Lee and Paula completed their courses at the Summer Institute of Linguistics in Seattle, were accepted as Members-in-Training with Wycliffe and moved to Dallas for further linguistic studies and their field training. Then to top off the year, in December 1985, I wrote in a newsletter that grandson Jonathan, age 3, had asked Jesus into his heart.

I remember well that it was in 1986 that Hugh began waking me up with his snoring in the early morning hours, and I was frustrated. Try as I might to get back to sleep, I couldn't. Anywhere between 3:30 and 5:00 a.m. was the bewitching hour. I'd lay in bed stewing morning after morning. Sometimes I fell back to sleep if I got up and went into one of the other bedrooms, but I didn't like doing that. Hugh decided to have this painful surgery on his palate to try to alleviate the situation, only to keep snoring as usual. He tried the nose strips guaranteed to stop snoring. They didn't. Then he got an expensive mouth guard that was supposed to keep his mouth open to let more air in, and while the snoring was less guttural, he would still wake me up even when I put in ear plugs.

As I lay there one morning, it was as if I heard God say, "Why not get up and spend some time with Me?"

I had always had "devotions" or a "quiet time." I loved meeting with the Lord in prayer and Bible reading. It wasn't always a disciplined regular time, however, and sometimes, in the crush of the day, especially when the children were small, the day would press in and, oops! The hours would somehow get away from me and I'd fall into bed at night and realize I hadn't even said "hello" to God that day. No wonder I got impatient. No wonder my temper had flared. No wonder I hadn't been alert to God-appointed interrupters. No wonder my actions and reactions had not been for the display of His splendor in any way, shape or form that day!

One day when Hugh awakened me at 4:00 a.m., I decided to get up and go into to the living room to meet God instead of stewing in my bed.

I don't know if my reading was in Isaiah that day or I just opened to it, but I read Isaiah 50:4:

> *The Sovereign Lord has given me an instructed tongue*
> *to know the word that sustains the weary.*

I was delighted to read that. I felt God had given me the gift of encouragement through my many cards and letters I'd send out month by month. I'm sure I had read that verse before, but this time I felt it was especially for me and I asked God to increase my ability to be sensitive to other's needs and that my words would indeed be from Him and bring encouragement.

I went back to Isaiah 50:4 and continued reading.

> *He wakens me morning by morning, wakens my ear to listen*
> *like one being taught.*

There's a Greek word we use in English to express "triumph in a discovery." It's *eureka!* It was indeed my "eureka" moment. I had been so consumed with the "how" of the situation—*how* can I get Hugh to stop snoring?—I almost missed the "what." *What* should I do with these early morning hours when I can't get back to sleep?

With promptings from God and this verse, the following morning when Hugh woke me up once more, I happily got up, went into the living room and had a wonderful visit with my Lord.

That was twenty-three years ago and meeting God at anywhere from 4:00 or 5:00 until 6:30 or 7:00 is as natural to me now as brushing my teeth. The only thing that's changed is with the children all gone, I now have a special place in one of the extra bedrooms with a comfy chair and all my devotional materials around me. And how do I fill my time? I can tell you it goes by quickly.

I write in my journal recalling what I did the day before (to keep my gray cells working). I write it as a letter to God and along with thanking him for yesterday's happenings, I thank and praise him for new truths learned from my Bible reading and/or devotional books. I sing hymns or praise songs. I learned this from our son-in-law, Greg Asimakoupoulos. It's a great devotional/worship tool. I've gone through hymnbooks singing all the old hymns I know. One of my favorites is the Inter-Varsity hymnbook that we used in Mexico for our Sunday night services at our headquarters. I also use a stack of praise hymns I've pulled out from Trinity's Sunday bulletins.

I read a daily devotional like *My Utmost for His Highest*, by Oswald Chambers. He also has several others: *Devotions for a Deeper Life, Still Higher for His Highest* and *A New Testament Walk with Oswald Chambers*. But I've also enjoyed over the years, *Streams in the Dessert*, compiled by Mrs. Charles E. Cowman, *Walking with God Day by Day* by Martyn Lloyd-Jones, *God's Best Secrets* by Andrew Murray,

Your Father Loves You by James Packer, *Living the Message* by Eugene H. Person, *Devotional Classics*, edited by Richard J. Foster and James Bryan Smith, and many others. And I go back after several years and use them again, although I use *My Utmost for His Highest* the most.

I usually read other books *on* prayer or books *of* prayers as part of my meeting with God. This year I'm reading one prayer a day from a book of Puritan Prayers edited by Arthur Bennett, the *Valley of Vision*. I've also enjoyed Madame Guyon, Fenelón, and Amy Carmichael's devotional books, and I found going through the *One Year Book of Personal Prayer*, of older and contemporary prayers by various people, and *Day by Day with the Early Church Fathers*, also a blessing.

Over the years I've written down prayers from Scripture, books and other resources that I find meaningful. I adapt them to use in praying for our family and pray a page or two daily. I've listed some of these in *Appendix II*.

As I write this, I'm going through the New Revised Standard Version *Renovarè Spiritual Formation Bible*. Earlier I used the *Daily Walk Bible* in the New Living Bible translation that is divided into daily portions to read through in a year. That was a special blessing. I've also used *The Women's Devotional Bible*, *The Message*, NIV in various editions, the Living Bible, Phillip's, and way back when, the King James Version because that was the only Bible I had. In order to keep fresh and not stagnate, I've found it important to vary the translations and devotional books I read.

I keep a prayer journal writing down requests and leaving a column for answers that I put in red ink. It's a wonderful encouragement to go back and see the many answers to prayer. And then over the week I pray through the weekly Presidential Prayer Bulletin, Trinity's Prayer Sheet and the prayer sheet from our adult Sunday School, King's Class. I print out the prayer requests that come on line from missionaries and others. Wycliffe sends out a bi-monthly sheet called "Intercessor," and I get daily Wycliffe requests on line as well.

Another important prayer list comes on line weekly from John Schaeffer who leads Bible studies for incarcerated young men at Juvenile Hall. I have a real burden for these needy young people as with everyone I bring before the Lord. It's such a rich privilege to be a partner with God in what He is doing in individual lives here and around the world. Recently I've been sending emails to John with specific prayers for the requests he sends out. He told me he's giving them to the young men and they apparently are encouraged to know someone is truly praying for them.

Now I understand not all will be able to or even want to follow my regimen. But for me, I know why God is waking me morning by morning, even without Hugh's snoring. He's calling me to visit with Him in prayer and to listen and be taught by Him.

It had been a full year but we had one more blessing in store for us in 1986 aside for the new offices over our garage I've already mentioned in Chapter 10. Lee and Paula arrived December 12 and spent Christmas with us before leaving for Wycliffe's field training course (formerly "Jungle Camp"). The extra room in the new offices was quickly put to good use when Wendy, Greg, Kristin and

. . . .

Allison arrived Christmas Day to spend Christmas with us as well.

January 1987 marked thirty years since we had left for Mexico. We numbered four when we left. Now we numbered fourteen. We had added two more children, two daughters-in-law, one son-in-law and five grandchildren. Hugh was working on his 21st book. The sequel to *Manuel* called *Manuel the Continuing Story* was out, as was *Behind the Story*, and he was working on a 20th anniversary volume for Wycliffe Associates. Lee and Paula left January 3rd and by February 3rd were a month into their field training course and had been assigned to the Maluku Islands (formerly the Spice Islands) in Indonesia. Karen was in China with the Chapman College Chamber Orchestra and I was still teaching Bible studies and active in Trinity's prayer ministry.

In September 1987, I once again had the opportunity to go with Hugh on one of his photo-journalism trips. I was still enchanted with getting to go abroad with him, but this was one of the trips that made me "almost" content to be a homebody! I would have one more in 1990 that would clinch it!

We left on September 21, 1987 at 3:00 a.m. on Qantas Airlines for Perth, Australia. Someone had said to be sure to dress warmly as it gets cold at that time of night. However, the rows in the 747 Jumbo Jet were pushed closer together than usual with an extra row added at the back of the front section. The other half of the plane had cargo.

· ·

Our seats were the two middle seats in the middle section of the last row.   And because there was not supposed to be a row of seats there, we didn't have air vents and our seats didn't recline. To make matters worse, the passengers on either side of us promptly went to sleep, and because our seats were so close to the row in front, to get out we had to climb over our seatmates on either side.

With a 21-hour flight ahead of us, we wanted to get up to get some exercise every now and then.   This was awkward but not as bad as roasting under a heavy sweatshirt. As I didn't have a blouse or shirt underneath, I couldn't remove it. I thought I'd melt.

Later we flew to Darwin in the north and Kangaroo Ground outside Melbourne in the south, and then went to two aboriginal areas.   Hugh taped interviews and took dozens of rolls of film and I enjoyed meeting and visiting with Wycliffe members and helping out where needed. I washed dishes, ironed, mended, and edited a linguistic paper.

We then flew to Vanuatu (formerly the New Hebrides), a country made up of 80 islands with 107 different languages. To get to the missionaries' home, we went in a jeep over unimaginable roads where I sat crunched over for a half hour in the back of the jeep, my head hitting the roof with every bump.   God was certainly showing me what I had been missing! But I will say that getting to see Scripture being translated and used was inspiring and a blessing. And getting in on a lap-lap, a feast spread on the ground on long rows of banana leaves that included manioc, fish, pumpkin, watermelon, taro, squash, bits of barbecued meat and sweet potatoes, was a once-in-a-lifetime experience. Especially since it was a celebration for three young men from three different language groups who had completed a course in translation principles. This enabled them to translate the New Testament in their own languages. It was a wonderful time of fellowship with our newly-met brothers and sisters in Christ, but I couldn't help but think of that jeep ride back!

The day we arrived back from Australia, Lee and Paula received their Indonesian visas and they left for Ambon on November 15.

In January 1988, I was elected to the Pastor Nominating Committee. Trinity was in need of an Associate Pastor and as vice-chairman, I gave a weekly devotional for the year we met. We eventually went through 123 thirteen-page dossiers before unanimously calling our candidate, Rev. Jim Christianson.

Karen gave a full flute recital for her Junior year. A week later she won first place in her division of the Musical Arts Club of Orange County competition. Along with her studies, she was teaching five flute students and singing and playing her flute for many weddings. She was also registered to go to the Johannesan International School of the Arts in Victoria, B.C. Canada for the summer.

It was also in this newsletter I wrote about feeling "absolutely inundated with letters to answer." This is probably a good time to write about the hundreds of letters I've written over these 52 years as missionaries with Wycliffe. On an average, I have written well over sixty letters or cards a month and since the advent of computers, I've lost count of the several emails I send out every day. Before computers, there were times when I thought I just couldn't write another letter, but I thank God for all our friends, and if at times my notes have been short, I hope if they get to read this book, they will understand the extent of our correspondence and why, at times, I feel inundated!

In this newsletter I also mentioned the joy of having led a young woman to Christ after the morning service. I have been part of Trinity's after-Sunday Worship Prayer Team for more than twenty years. I led it for several years, scheduling two or three pray-ers each Sunday after our two morning services and taking one Sunday service as well. I finally gave over the leadership a couple of years ago as I felt I was over-involved and it was becoming too stressful for me. I especially was grateful not to have the responsibility when we added a third Sunday morning service and needed pray-ers for that service as well.

Lee and Paula wrote to tell us they were rejoicing that they had been "sent by God to work among the Romans in the village of Jerusu." (Sounds like something biblical, doesn't it?)

They ended by telling us some sad news about the

Lee and Paula's assignment to the village of Jerusu on the Island of Roma, Indonesia, six days by boat from Ambon.

possibility of having to leave Indonesia at the end of 1990 when the government said they would no longer issue or renew visas. In the meantime, however, they asked prayer for their good health to continue "because emergency medical help is almost nil." To get to their field assignment it took four days by boat and they asked that we pray for an amphibious plane for Wycliffe's work in the Maluku Islands. By plane their long boat trip could be cut to 1 ½ hours. They later asked us to send life jackets as the rickety boat on which they traveled didn't provide them.

I also need to mention that during these years we enjoyed having Kristi and Dave and the children as Trinity members and seeing them every Sunday. Kristi was active in the women's ministry and along with being the chairwoman of the Wycliffe Missions Sub-committee, she also was the accompanist for a children's choir Karen led. Dave, at this time, had begun a two-year course to become a Bethel Bible Study Leader and I also had the fun of taking a three-day course with him at Calvary Church in Santa Ana entitled, "The Seven Laws of the Learner Seminar" designed to hone our teaching and communication skills.

Hugh was finishing his 22nd book, *Pike's Perspectives*, and we made plans for our vacation, driving up to Canada in our new used car, an '85 Olds Cutlass replacing our '74 Chevrolet. Before going to Thetis, we would drop off Karen in Victoria for a course at the Johannesen International School of the Arts. She had recently won two flute competitions with monetary awards and these were a great help toward enabling her to do this. It was a special summer for us. The "Steven Motel" hosted friends from

....

Alaska, Vanuatu, Australia, Indonesia and Tennessee and we were able to have extended time in Canada visiting over 100 friends along with two weeks at Thetis. Our whole family, except for Lee and Paula, were also able to be with us for four days. Karen joined us after she finished her course in Victoria. She stayed with us in the A-Frame and the rest of the family stayed at Capernwray on Thetis, and came over to fish and beach comb during the day. Hugh caught the most fish ever and had great fun teaching the grandchildren to fish with the new poles he bought them. We missed Lee and Paula and felt especially sorry to hear, when we got home, that their camera was stolen as well as their passports and other important papers.

Karen gave her senior recital February 18, 1989, with Wendy, Dave, Kristi, several college friends and our friends in attendance.

In March 1989, Hugh was working on a new book from material we gathered more than a year ago in the South Pacific, but I wrote that he was constantly interrupted by final corrections on his latest book, *Pike's Perspectives*.

Before the advent of computers and digital desktop publishing, getting a manuscript out the door to the publisher was an enormous task. Hugh would write it out it longhand after transcribing huge amounts of text from taped interviews. I would sometimes type a manuscript three and four times because after editing there were new paragraphs to include or move around, spelling mistakes to fix, and sentences to rewrite. Then I'd proofread the whole book before someone else proofread it and off we sent it to the publisher. No wonder someone said at that time, publishing a book was like giving birth to a bale of barbed wire! With typesetters working on the manuscript,

. . . .

often new mistakes were introduced and another whole process of proof reading and correcting the galley sheets they sent back would take place. And we haven't even talked about someone designing a cover! After all that, when we picked up the finished product, invariably we'd discover a typo after a few lines. Needless to say we rejoice that books, while still a lot of work, are much easier to produce these days!

Wendy and Greg were also asking for prayer as they were in the throes of seeking God's will. After eleven years at Crossroads Covenant Church, they felt God was leading them elsewhere. Four or five other churches in various locations were interested in them, and it looked like we would be losing their close proximity to us.

On May 28 Karen graduated summa cum laude from Chapman College with her Music Performance degree and also asked prayer for God's clear direction for the summer and coming year. She had eight flute students and was hoping to increase this number and have an increase in engagements (gigs) where she could use her talents as a flutist and vocalist.

It was around this time a woman from The Best Sellers Publish Co. contacted me and asked if I would be interested in writing a children's daily devotional for a perpetual calendar. Her idea was to have a prayer poem and Bible verse to go with it on each page. The only catch was she needed it done in one month. I started to rhyme morning, noon and night, but it soon became apparent I could in no way write 365 prayer poems by the end of the month. I asked if I could half it and write 183 prayer-poems (the one extra for a leap year) and the Bible verse to go with it could be on the next page. She agreed.

She paid me ten dollars for each prayer poem and each Bible verse. No royalties, just a one-time check for $3,650.00. We knew what we would use it for. We were going to use it to get our house air conditioned!

At the end of the month, I had completed my assignment. My perpetual calendar for children ages 5-11 was titled, "365 Prayers and Bible Verses for Children," and it was shrink-wrapped with another perpetual calendar of Bible stories written by another author titled, "365 Bible Stories for Children." These sold in Costco until they were sold out. I was hopeful they would reprint it but it wasn't to be. Years later I wrote another 182 prayer poems with Bible verses so that each day would have a prayer-poem and Bible verse. I tried to have the book republished, but without success. We did have our air conditioning, however, and for that we were most grateful.

One of my favorite prayer-poems in my little book was the one I wrote for February 14:

> Thank you, God, for hugs.
> They are a nice invention.
> They make me feel so loved
> I think that's their intention!

The Bible verse to go with that one was John 13:34, "A new command I give you: Love one another. As I have loved you, so you must love one another."

I tried to cover subjects suitable for children as well as things to avoid like "gossip."

Forgive me when I gossip,
Or tell a tale or two,
For if I tell on others
I'm not a friend that's true.

The Bible verse for this one on March 2 was: "A gossip betrays a confidence; so avoid a man [person] who talks too much" (Proverbs 20:19).

Under the title, "When Pets Die," I wrote:

Sometimes the pets we love get old,
It makes us sad they die,
Sometimes they get run over
And we cry and wonder why.
But help us to be thankful
For the fun when they were here.
It's hard, we really miss them,
But it helps when You are near.

June 11 had the verse to go with this from 2 Corinthians 1:3: "Praise be to the God and Father of our Lord Jesus Christ, the Father of compassion and the God of all comfort."

It was interesting to me that older people liked the daily devotional. One older person told me she liked the large printing, and because she could stand the book up on her table, she could look at the poem or Bible verse several times a day. Because the devotional was brief, it was something she could remember all day.

Mothers told me it was just the right amount with which to send off their children to school, and the prayer-poems

. . . .

often led to discussions about the emphasis for that day. But no matter. Like other materials I've written and not published, it's still languishing in my file cabinet! Who knows? One day I might just dust off some of these things and try again.

15

When God Speaks, People
Ministry, Battle

In 1988, Karen was still living at home. She continued
to teach her flute students ranging in ages from 8 to
over 60. She was also leading one of Trinity's children's
choirs, she sang in Trinity's adult choir and was a co-
leader of a post-college Bible study. When we moved to
Santa Ana in 1970, Karen was only three. She loved to take
walks with Hugh in and around all the orange groves.
They had long since been replaced with town houses and
apartments, but Karen still liked a Sunday afternoon walk
and I was always happy to join her. This particular
Sunday she wanted to know about a recent incident with
our neighbor.

"I know you said God told you to write a letter," she
said, "but how did that come about?"

"I'd been up in my office studying James for some
studies I was giving," I said, "and had been reading in
James 2:14 where he asks, 'What good is faith without
action?' James tells us not to just tell our friend in need to
have a good day and stay warm and well. We're supposed
to give them some tangible help."

"I know that passage," Karen said, "but what did that
have to do with Sherry?"

"You know how as a single parent she never has enough
for house repairs, and I had just read that passage and

. . . .

came out on the small office porch that overlooks her roof and remembered she told me it was leaking. Out loud I said, 'Now God, what are we supposed to do about this? We can hardly take care of our own house repairs. How are we supposed to get Sherry a new roof?' And that's when I heard or had an impression of God telling me to write a letter."

"I don't think I've heard God say anything that clearly to me," said Karen.

"It hasn't happened that often," I said.

Karen jogged religiously every morning and the next day she was out running her usual route. About a block away she noticed two bills folded into neat one-inch squares on the side of the sidewalk. She picked them up, unfolded them, and in her hand she held two ten dollar bills, a wonderful find for a "starving musician." She tucked them into her sock and kept running. When she got to a main street, there stood a Mexican woman obviously pregnant with three stair-step children in tow. And that's when she heard, "Give the money to the lady." She was sure she was hearing things and kept right on running past the woman and her children until she got to the end of the block. And that's when she heard it again. "Give the money to the lady." She realized this time, it was from God and she turned around, ran back and did what she believed God had told her to do. It was a beautiful moment for her and when she told me about it later, she was glowing.

My neighbor, who needed a new roof, attended a nearby church. Obeying my nudge, I wrote a letter to the pastor, explaining that one of their members was my neighbor and she was in great need of a new roof. I also mentioned that perhaps this might be a great project for one of their small groups. I thought it might help if I told him I was a member of Wycliffe Bible Translators (to give me some credence!) and that our son Dave would be happy to be part of the work crew. Then, as an added incentive, I added that I would be willing to feed lunch to the group for as long as it took them. I sent off the letter and prayed daily someone would pick up the challenge.

Six weeks went by and I hadn't heard a thing. I began to feel a little foolish. Maybe I had just thought in my mind I should write a letter. Maybe it hadn't been a command from the Lord after all. But, no, I knew how clearly I had been impressed to write a letter.

Finally I had a phone call from one of the associate pastors apologizing he had taken so long to do anything about my letter. "I was crossing the patio last Sunday," he said, "and one of our members asked me if there wasn't something their small group could do other than going out to eat all the time. I had your letter still in my suit jacket and I pulled it out and said, 'I've got just the thing for you.' The long and short of it is, a couple of the men are coming over to check it out to see what materials we need. We'll get the supplies and hopefully be able to start in a week. Could you let your neighbor know?"

I did as I had promised. I fed the crew of twelve to fifteen men, including our son Dave, on the weekend, Thursday, Friday and Saturday, on our patio. What a sight it was to see all of them working together. I knew these men were blessed as they put action to their faith. And every time I went up to my office, I looked at the roof, smiled and thanked God I didn't have to tell Sherry,

"Sorry about your roof, but stay well and hopefully we won't get too much rain."

There was one last letter from Lee and Paula to close out 1989. They wrote that they had both had malaria but in spite of this, they had translated a storybook and songbook in the Roma language.

I had the fun of having Wycliffe publish two of my Vacation Bible School programs I had written for Trinity's VBS with an emphasis on missions. One was titled *Carey's Shoe Store*; the other, *The Castle—Jesus is King.* Hugh was sifting through mountains of material for another book on the life and times of William Cameron Townsend that would eventually be the second book of four. In a newsletter I asked for "stamina, creativity and patience" for him.

On September 17, Hugh's mother passed away and we made a quick trip to Canada. The funeral was in Vancouver as she would be buried beside Hugh's dad. Greg officiated and brought comfort to us all. Just two months before she died, we had said our good-byes with tears as we knew it was near the end. And when the end came, we were glad she had been freed from her terrible pain she had endured through countless operations and chemo treatments. She had made a profession of faith some years earlier and we knew she was with the Lord.

In December 1990 we sent out Christmas greetings and shared that in September we had "twenty young people attend our writers' workshop in Singapore and fifty in Australia, eighteen from other missions. We made many friends, helped would-be and published authors, shared devotional thoughts in three chapel times, plus two other gatherings, and were ourselves refreshed."

We also announced Wendy and Greg's third child, our sixth grandchild, Lauren Star, born on November 15, 1990. Lee and Paula returned the next day from Indonesia since they were unable to renew their visas and their first child was due in February. This meant we could all be together to celebrate American Thanksgiving! And to finish our busy year, we praised God that Hugh's new book, *A Candle in the Dark,* was finally published.

Grandchild number seven, Walker Zachary Steven, arrived in Dallas, Texas on February 17, 1991. Lee and Paula had settled there for a furlough year, to await the baby, and for Lee to finish his MA in linguistics. For his thesis he used the Roma language data that he and Paula had gathered while in Indonesia. Paula had a malaria attack the day after Walker was born but she didn't let that slow her down. After her recovery she wrote, "In between changing diapers, I'm organizing our mounds of field notes into dictionary form."

The year 1991 was a year of milestones:
--40 years since Wycliffe's first New Testament was published
--Hugh and I turned 60
--We had our 40th wedding anniversary
--It was our 35th anniversary as Wycliffe members
--*They Dared to be Different* went into a third printing, and
--30 Soviet students signed up for a month-long translation course in Moscow

. . . .

It was noon on a lovely warm, sunny summer day. Time for lunch, and Hugh offered to make it as I had worked all morning answering correspondence.

He called me when lunch was ready. I pushed back my chair from my desk, stretched my weary bones, and went out on the porch outside Hugh's office. Hugh had our lunch all nicely laid out on the picnic table on the patio and was waiting for me with a pile of mail that had just been delivered, which in itself was unusual. Our mail usually came around 3:30 in the afternoon.

As I walked wearily down the stairs to the patio, I said, "Oh, I'm so sick and tired of staring at my computer screen all day. I think I'd like a people ministry!"

"Maybe your wish is going to come true," said Hugh. "Read this."

It was a letter from one of our "summertime friends," Ken Smith, who was now back home in Vancouver and heavily involved in the work at their church, Granville Chapel.

I read the letter and screamed (my usual reaction when excited). "I can't believe it!" I said. "We've been wondering how to help my sisters with my father's care and this sounds like it might be just what we need, to say nothing of a people ministry!"

In the letter, Ken Smith wrote that Granville Chapel was considering adding to their staff in the area of pastoral care. "It would be part-time," he wrote. "We need a friendly couple like yourselves to interact with our seniors and be able to train others."

I couldn't contain my wonder at this letter coming at that moment I had expressed a desire for a "people ministry." Surely this was made to order by God!

We talked it over with the family and they jokingly said, "This sounds like a job for Mother, but how about you, Dad?" They knew over the years of his writing career he had become more and more content with himself and in many ways had become a loner—something needful if one is going to be disciplined to get up every day and sit at a desk staring at a blank sheet of paper, waiting for inspiration to come!

They also knew I felt a responsibility toward my dad. It was not an easy trek for my sisters who lived on Vancouver Island. Often it would take six hours—longer if they missed a ferry—to go from their house to Dad's. The more we talked and prayed Hugh began to sense that this was what God was giving us to do. But there were still things to consider.

Karen needed someone to stay with her in our home. No problem. It "just happened" two of her friends, Betty Saadeh (now Christiansen) and Angela Dienhart (now Hancock) were available to move in with her. Then we had the wonderful news that Wycliffe had asked Lee and Paula to teach linguistics for the summer of 1992 to new recruits at the Canadian Institute of Linguists (CanIL) held at Trinity Western University in Langley, B.C., a little over an hour away from where we'd be. We could get together weekends.

We wrote Ken to set a date for us to be interviewed and meet the folks at Granville, which we did. It was a great meeting. We knew they would interview others, but we felt such a kindred spirit with everyone.

An interesting thing happened after we shared our testimonies and were having refreshments. I was talking with a tall, distinguished man who told me he and his wife

Lila had been missionaries in India. For some reason I twigged to his wife's name and I asked him if her maiden name had been Shields. "Why yes," he said. I almost fainted. Forty-two years earlier, Hugh had taken me to an inter-Varsity beach party with his friends. We were newly dating and I felt uncomfortable and insecure not knowing anyone. It probably showed in my face. And then this university student with a beautiful smile on her face came up to me and started talking to me. I never forgot her name or her kindness and we often mentioned her over the years when talking about the importance of reaching out to new people. Her name? Lila Shields. She never knew the impact she had on me and now after all these years I could tell her.

She didn't remember me, of course, but I was happy to get the opportunity to thank her. And then she told me her husband, a retired missionary doctor with whom I had been talking, had Alzheimer's. I never sensed that in any way when I was talking to him. He was completely coherent. I felt it was God's gift to me and another affirmation that this is where we should be. Dr. Gilmore Davies passed away while we were there and Hugh was asked to take his funeral.

A couple of weeks after we returned back home we received a formal invitation to come on staff at Granville Chapel. We had to inform them that we couldn't come until October as Hugh had a photo shoot in Mexico. This was fine with them and it gave us time to think about what to do about housing in Canada.

We decided to put out a letter to our Canadian friends stating our need and almost immediately we received a call from Zoe Wong with whom I had worked at the

. . . .

Health Unit before I was married. Zoe, a Public Health Nurse, and her husband Bill, a tailor, had become our friends before we left for Mexico in 1957 and on some of our trips up to Vancouver in the summer, we had visited them to catch up on each other and our families, and they had also visited us in Santa Ana.

She told us her daughter had an empty house for rent in East Vancouver for $1200.00 a month. "Oh-h-h," I said, "I don't think we can afford more than $1000.00 a month on our budget." She agreed to that immediately and sight unseen we contracted to rent it.

After we arrived, I wrote in November 1991, "What a pleasant surprise to discover a unique five-level home with a wonderful kitchen, a dining area, a nook for a desk, three bedrooms and ample room for hospitality. It's been a challenge to beg, borrow or buy second-hand furniture to furnish it. We still lack some items but it already feels like home."

It was indeed a unique house. Situated on a narrow lot, it covered it all except for a small patch of green in the back. The front entrance was a few steps from the sidewalk. When one walked in, to the right was a room we used for our bedroom. Down eight steps was the basement and laundry. Up eight steps was a bathroom and around the corner the kitchen, desk space and dining area; up eight steps was the living room, and up another eight steps were two bedrooms and another bathroom.

Needless to say, this was exactly the house I didn't need for my propensity to fall down steps. And, of course, I did fall down one set of stairs twice and have lumpy ankles as a reminder! But seriously, we were grateful to all who helped us furnish the house and especially to Ken and

Ruth Smith who bought our bed and Ruth, an artist, who filled our bare walls with her framed watercolors turning our house into a home.

Hugh had hoped to work on the second volume of Uncle Cam's life, but he soon discovered with my dad's care and pastoral care, it was impossible. And while our job description said "half time," often we had full days with little time left for writing.

At first we went out to Maple Ridge, about an hour from Vancouver, twice a week. Our days were filled from morning to night. with banking, shopping, cleaning and just getting rid of piles of old cereal boxes, TV dinner containers and newspapers.   For weeks we'd load up our truck and take things to the dump or recycling center. We never knew, when we bought our Toyota truck just before going to Canada, what a wonderful help it would be.

When we were deciding what kind of vehicle we should get to transport our household goods to Vancouver, Hugh looked around at various dealerships, but a week before we were to leave, he still hadn't made a decision. On the Monday morning before we were to leave on Thursday, the Lord seemed to strongly indicate to Hugh he should get the Toyota truck, and he bought it with confidence that it was the right thing to do. Indeed it was!

At Christmas we flew down to Wendy and Greg's in Concord, California for a week where all sixteen of us had been able to congregate. It was the first time in five years we had all been together for Christmas. How we savored that time together!

Lee received his Masters in Linguistics just before Christmas, and after their return to Texas, he continued to teach linguistics to Wycliffe's new recruits at the linguistic center in Dallas. They were looking forward to their summer assignment in Canada, and Karen, Dave, Kristi and the boys were all planning to come up the beginning of July for a week.

In a March 1992 newsletter, I wrote:

> It's been a great challenge for us to minister in the area of pastoral care at Granville Chapel. We gave a seven-week course on "How to Build a Caring Fellowship" and we almost have three teams in place for welcoming, hospitality and caring. The response has been great and we praise God for all those who signed up to participate."

This was amazing as it was a new experience for Granville members. Up until recently, all services had been "lay led." Granville's roots were "Open" Plymouth Brethren, but they were now moving more toward becoming a community church. They had a secretary, Senior Pastor Tim MacIntosh, and us as pastoral care staff, but that was it. The committees we established were also a new concept so we wondered if we could "rally the troops." In our newsletter we thanked our friends for their prayers. God had been with us every step of the way in answer to them.

I ended the newsletter with, "We've also had a lot of one on one interaction and our home has been overflowing with dinner, lunch and overnight guests."

We originally thought our ministry would be mostly to seniors, but we were happy for our involvement with university students and young adults as this gave us opportunities to present Wycliffe as a possible avenue for mission service.

· ·

My dad's care continued to be a concern. He was getting weaker and having more and more difficulty walking. I noticed he started to wear his slippers all the time so I asked him if he needed to get his doctor to look at his feet.

"I just need my nails cut," he grumbled.

I was sorry I had not thought this might be a problem for him. Because he couldn't bend down to take care of them himself, they were a mess. His nails had grown completely over his toes and were cutting into his toes underneath. It was a long process for me to soak and cut his nails but soon they were looking normal once more, and he got back into his shoes.

While this was a distasteful, hard task for me, it wasn't nearly as hard as what my mother had asked me to do shortly before she passed away. I had only known her to wear her long hair one way her whole life—pulled back in a bun she knotted at the nape of her neck. This was Mama as far as all of us were concerned.

But one day, when I came up to help with her care, she asked me to cut her hair. "I can't take care of it any longer," she said.

"Oh, Mama," I said, "don't ask me to do that."

"Yes," she said resolutely, "what must be, must be."

There was no getting out of it once Mama had made up her mind. I put a towel around her thin shoulders, brushed out her beautiful, long silver hair that she always braided before going to bed, and began, tears filling my eyes. Snip! At least six inches came off. Snip! Another six inches. Soon the kitchen floor was covered with hair clippings. It was now chin length and she asked for a mirror.

"You'll have to take off more yet," she said matter-of-factly. Tears were streaming down my face. She was so brave. How hard that must have been for her, but she never shed a tear. I kept cutting until it got to just above her chin. To me, it didn't look like my dear mother, but she got up, gave me a big hug, thanked me, and went to stretch out on her Lazy Boy chair.

But that was then, and now it was my dad's turn to receive some care and along with cutting his finger nails and toe nails, I also cut his hair regularly while we were there.

One day I decided to get up extra early to cook him a beef roast with potatoes and carrots and a homemade pie. In spite of our often-strained relationship, I was happy to be doing this knowing it would please him, and the Lord.

We usually walked in the front door but this time it was locked. Hugh banged on the door but there was no answer. We went around to the back door. Still no answer. I called through the front mail slot, and when there was no answer, we began to fear the worst.

A couple of weeks before this, on March 7th, we had celebrated his 90th birthday. My three sisters, even my oldest sister whom I hadn't seen in ten years since my mother's funeral, were there along with Dad's youngest brother Albert and his wife Ruth. There were eighteen in all including some grandchildren and great grandchildren. We had all chipped in and given him what he wanted--a gold pocket watch.

My sister had written to British Columbia's premier, the lieutenant governor and Dad's Member of Parliament and they all sent letters of congratulations. It was a rare happy

. . . .

time and he seemed to be stable and much stronger than when we first came in October 1991.

Had he taken a turn for the worse? Had he died in his bed? I looked through the living room window to see if I could see anything, and there was my dad lying motionless on the sofa right under the picture window. We both banged on the window, but he didn't move. Almost in a whisper I said, hardly believing it, "I think he's dead. I can't see him breathing. Maybe you should try to get in the back window?"

Hugh was on his way around the back, when I looked in the window again. Dad was nowhere in sight! I called Hugh to come back and we banged on the front door and again asked him to open the door, but there was no sound from within.

Now I was angry! My blood pressure was up from the shock of thinking he was dead when all along he'd been pretending. I bent down and yelled through the mail slot.

"For heaven's sake, Dad, open this door!" No answer. "I've brought you a lovely dinner. What's the matter with you?" No answer.

I was livid. I banged and banged on the door and said, "I'm not leaving until you let me in."

This time he said, "Get away from here. You've been robbing me blind. I've got a gun."

For the life of us we couldn't figure out what he was talking about, but we knew he had a rifle and if mad enough, he just might shoot through the door. We backed off, walked to our truck and talked about what we should do. It seemed best to leave and I suggested we go to the Social Service office to see if we could talk to his social worker. It sounded like my dad was losing it.

His particular social worker wasn't in, but I talked with the director who kindly listened to me as, through my tears, I told him my tale of woe. He suggested we go out for lunch and then call Dad to tell him we were coming over. "I'm sure by then he'll be fine," he assured us.

We did as he suggested. When I called Dad, he was calm and collected. I asked him for his grocery list and we bought his needed items and went back. I was still not too kindly disposed toward him when he opened the door. I greeted him with a cool, "Hello," and took the meal into the kitchen. Hugh followed with the groceries. I then turned unsmilingly to him and said, "Okay, what's this all about?"

I was sixty-one. I had never raised my voice to my father my whole life, nor ever confronted him about his aberrant behavior because I felt his anger would just make things worse. But now I was ready for battle.

He walked over, without a word, to the china cabinet and pointed to the empty shelves. "You've stolen my dishes," he said.

"What are you talking about? You let me take them to use while we're here," I said.

"So you say," he said.

"What is it with you?" I asked. "I should think if your daughter needed dishes and you had an old set you weren't using, you'd be happy to let her have them."

"They're my dishes," he said, "and if I want to keep them or sell them at an auction, I can."

"Oh, I give up!" I said. "I can't understand you. I've never understood you. You don't know how to be a father!"

"And you don't know how to be a daughter," he said with a sheepish smile.

He knew at that point, I believe, he had indeed let me have them but had forgotten. Nevertheless, I wasn't ready to be chummy. This was just one time too many. I put his groceries away, told him to heat the meal in the oven, and said we'd be back in a week. And I went away knowing I'd have to deal with another one of those "seventy-seven" times I'd have to forgive him with God's help.

As 1992 closed, we felt, in spite of difficulties with my father, it had been a rich year with new challenges, new friends, many, many visitors, including our family, and many and varied opportunities for ministry.

16

Homegoings, Going Home, New Relatives

Lee and Paula had one more summer with us. They would be back in Canada teaching linguistics and we'd have several weeks to enjoy their weekend visits once again. Walker had been such fun the previous summer when in the early morning he'd stand on the 5th level at the top of the stairs outside Lee and Paula's bedroom yelling, "Ya-ya-ya-ya" hoping we'd hear him and come to get him. Which we did, and Lee and Paula, who had slipped him out of the room, would go back to sleep.

Now at two he was learning new words every day. We were looking forward to them coming in from Langley during the week, as they had done the previous summer, to enjoy those long, light summer evenings when the sun wouldn't set until 9:30. On those occasions, we'd meet them at Spanish Banks for fish and chips. As I write this, I smile. Those times are still happy memories for me.

Our plan was to return to Santa Ana the end of August 1993 when Lee and Paula would fly back to Dallas. We'd been able to set in place more care for my dad and soon we only needed to go out once a week. Someone was shopping for his groceries, two homemakers were coming twice a day to wash his clothes or clean his house. They'd make two meals and he could get his own breakfast. Another person would take him to the bank and others

. . . .

were coming to cut his hair and nails. My sisters Eileen and Shirley would also be coming over from time to time, and since he was so much better than when we first arrived, we felt at ease about leaving him.

We still felt he would be better off in a care home, but he adamantly refused. We had been urged to get Power of Attorney, but again we were unsuccessful.

Christmas 1992 Karen came to celebrate with us—a special joy! During this time she shared she felt she should go back to university to get her elementary teacher's certificate as she just wasn't making it with her music. It saddened us, as music was her passion. Going back to school meant she would have to give up her flute students, her part-time job teaching music to grades 3-6 in a private school, and leading a choir at Trinity—all things she loved, but she didn't want to live at home the rest of her life!

She was able to get all her transcripts together when she returned and was once again a student, this time at the University of California at Irvine.

This also meant she could not keep up the garden like she had. She hired some gardeners who were cutting lawns at the neighbors, and to this day, we still use them. It was great having them in place when we returned because Hugh's arthritic back and knees were making it impossible for him to do what he had done before.

In a letter dated May 20, 1993, I received a lovely letter from my sister Shirley that reminded me of an evening forty-eight years earlier when she was ten and I was fourteen. She wrote:

> Today is a very special day. Forty-eight years ago on May 20th, I gave my heart to the Lord after you had

talked to me about it.   What a difference that decision has made in my life. We have experienced so much of the Lord's grace, and His goodness in our lives is overwhelming. So thank you, dear Sister, for speaking to me that night so long ago, prompting me to follow the Lord...a decision I have never regretted.

I'm so glad I saved Shirley's letter. It blessed me as much today in 2009 as it did when she first sent it in 1993.

As it came time for us to say good-bye to our dear friends at Granville, we were leaving with wonderful memories of some of the greatest friendships we've ever made. We still correspond with several of these friends.

We arrived home in Santa Ana the end of August and Hugh was back at his desk working on the second volume of Uncle Cam's life. He was encouraged to learn that his book *To the Ends of the Earth* was being used in Trinidad to educate people about the importance of Bible translation and a new recruitment office they were setting up. And in the meantime we were also encouraged with what we had been able to accomplish in the almost two years at Granville. In our December 1993 letter we enclosed in our Christmas cards, I wrote:

Before we left Granville Chapel, we were able to set up a system for keeping attendance, a home-bound buddy system, a welcoming team, hospital/home care team, and a bereavement team. I established a Bible study for young mothers, headed a prayer chain ministry and wrote a pastoral care handbook and pamphlet outlining opportunities for ministry with corresponding spiritual gifts. The amazing thing about all this is that as we trained others, God moved others to take over the leadership of all these ministries and we left with a feeling of "mission accomplished."

Our arrival back home was hard on Karen. She had had the run of the house. Now all her decorative items and other possessions were relegated to her bedroom. In January 1994, at age 26, she was itching to get a place of her own. She was still studying, but she was able to get into an intern practice teaching position in Irvine where she had 32 third graders and she was happily playing her flute for weddings on the weekends. Shortly later she was able to rent a one-bedroom plus loft condo in Irvine and happily settled in.

By April 1994, Shirley was able to get Dad's consent to go into a care home in Victoria, B.C. near her home. It was a relief for us all. At 92 he was no longer able to live on his own. My sisters and I and our spouses gathered to clean out Dad's house and out buildings to get it ready for selling. We were grateful to Al, Shirley's husband, for getting a good price at the right time. The money was deposited to be used for Dad's care.

In late summer, Lee and Paula and Wendy and Greg and their families came to Santa Ana for a vacation and we realized firsthand that life does indeed hang by a slender thread. We were all at Newport Beach one evening when an unusual wave slammed Greg into the sand. He sustained a sprained neck. We were sobered to learn that he came within a hair's breadth of breaking his neck. His injury came at a time when he had just accepted a call to Naperville Covenant Church in Illinois. He preached his first sermon there October 2nd, going before the rest of the family because their house in Concord, California hadn't sold. We were sad to see them leave California but happy they were being obedient to what God was giving them to do.

Although it was expected, it was still hard to learn that on July 14, 1995 we lost Al Lee, Shirley's husband, to liver cancer, at the age of 60. Three weeks later, my dad passed away on August 9 at 93 ½ years of age. Of all my sisters, Shirley had not experienced a lot of Dad's harshness. She grieved not only the loss of her husband of 37 years, but also our dad's passing.

Still grieving, a week after Al's death Shirley visited dad. She couldn't hold a conversation with him as his speech was slurred, so she'd sing old hymns. One day while she was singing hymns to him, he commented, "Yes, Jesus is the One to trust." He seemed to be in great pain a lot of the time and would yell loudly and groan. Shirley felt he was grieving as she herself had groaned similarly after her husband's death. I wondered, however, if he was grieving over his past life, so many years spent in resentment, bitterness and anger. The Psalmist wrote about this in Psalm 90:9 when he said, "All our days pass away under Your wrath; *we finish our years with a moan*" (italics added).

It was during these days of his loud moans that one day Shirley cried out, "O Lord Jesus, please take him home,' and Dad said, "Yes! Yes!" Shirley took the opportunity to ask him point blank if he had ever asked Jesus to forgive his sin. Dad answered, "Yes, I'm trusting in Jesus."

I had prayed for my father's salvation for sixty years. Countless others had also prayed for him as well. I praise God for His mercy in bringing Dad to himself. Isaiah 65:1 says: "I [God] reveal myself to those who did not ask for Me; I was found by those who did not seek Me." We believe Dad found peace with Jesus at the end of his earthly life and was welcomed by our gracious, loving, forgiving and compassionate Savior into Heaven.

Hugh took the service. Only my sisters and Dad's youngest brother and wife, plus a few of the grandchildren were there. I confess, I never shed a tear.

In reflection about my father, I realize when I see him again he will be changed. As we read in 1 John 3:2, "Dear friends, now we are children of God, and what we will be has not yet been made known. But we know that when He appears, we shall be like Him, for we shall see Him as He is."

Sometimes, I wonder, what will my changed father be like?

In 2009, I was blessed by a comment Murray Andrew Pura made on the *Parable of the Great Dinner* (Luke 14:16-24) in the NRSV Spiritual Formation Bible. He writes:

> We have often been told we will be surprised by the sort of people who will populate the Kingdom of Heaven. It is actually easier to imagine all sorts of street people being there then some of...our own personal enemies and people who slandered, assaulted or crushed us. Yet the God of Surprises will undoubtedly baffle us...by the sheer extravagance and inclusiveness of His grace. No sooner do we write off an individual than we can be

. . . .

sure God is working light and spirit into all the crevices and fissures of that person's soul."

Truly this is what God did in my father's soul, and I praise Him that I shall see my dad again, changed into His likeness. What a wonder!

While Hugh was back writing, I, too, was keeping my hand in it. I was writing a monthly column on prayer for Trinity's newsletter and now and then having an article or poem published. I also wrote a monthly column for Wycliffe Associates entitled, "Across my Kitchen Table," and I began leading a Bible study in James for our church seniors from material I had researched and written. I had taken over from our Associate Pastor who had left, and what I thought was to be a three-month weekly study turned into three years of weekly studies.

At the end of 1994, Lee and Paula proudly announced the arrival of our 8th grandchild, Isabel Marie, born December 17. We would see her in February when we went to Dallas to celebrate Walker's 4th birthday.

I need to mention Paula's creativity in making the most wonderful birthday parties for their children. This one had a castle and knight theme. She and Lee always dressed up in regalia to go with the theme whether it was medieval, pirates or Harry Potter! What wonderful memories they've given their three children.

Wendy and Greg had settled in Naperville, Illinois. It snowed on Halloween. Quite a shock! I remembered how shocked we were when we left Mexico and it snowed on Halloween when we moved to Buffalo Grove, Illinois.

None of us had mittens, scarves, warm coats or boots. We took care of that at Penny's, however, the next Saturday.

With four children to outfit on our budget, it was not easy. Wendy was 15 and wanting the latest fashions like any other teenager. When she had to have a pair of knitted gloves instead of the fur-lined leather ones, compliant as usual, she said, "That's okay."

Unknown to us, a clerk had heard her reply and when we got up to the cash register, she expressed her surprise that Wendy had not made a fuss.

"That's not what I usually hear," she said.

"Well, we're missionaries," I said. "We've just been reassigned here from Mexico. She knows that complaining won't do any good with four children to outfit."

The clerk's face brightened and she said, "Say, listen. My daughter just moved to Florida. She's about your daughter's size and I'm sure some of her winter clothes she left would fit her. Here's my address. Come by and we'll see what we can find."

The next Saturday we went to the woman's home and she not only gave Wendy a beautiful camel coat, but sweaters and other outfits as well. Then she pulled out some electrical appliances, blankets, and several other things and insisted we take them. We were overwhelmed. We had never met her before and never did again, but surely she was an angel, sent by God, to "supply all our needs (and more) according to His riches in glory."

By January 1996, Hugh's second volume on the life and times of William Cameron Townsend, *Wycliffe in the Making,* had finally come out. Wycliffe dedicated its 400th New Testament in the Barai language of Papua New

Guinea. A wonderful piece of news, but we had some happy news, too. Karen announced her engagement to Chris Romig (actually on November 3, 1995) and their wedding date was set for August 10, 1996. Like Karen, Chris was an accomplished musician (piano and organ) and was at Princeton Seminary. Yes, we were going to have another pastor in the family! The other good news was that Walker and Isabel were going to get a new brother. Grandchild #9 and child #3 for Lee and Paula was coming in June.

I was starting another 12-week study for the seniors. Hugh was looking into the possibility of another book project and we were rejoicing in God's goodness and provision for our needs. We were always aware how much our donors were a part of our work. Without them we could not continue what we believed to be God's assignment.

Marshall Sinclair Steven, third child for Lee and Paula and our 9th grandchild, put in his appearance on June 10, 1996. Lee had completed his first year of law school at the University of Virginia and was working that summer with a local law research firm. Lee's overseas' experience was put to good use when he graduated two years later and began working in international law with the law firm of White & Case in Washington, D.C.

The other big news, of course was Chris and Karen's wedding on August 10. It was a beautiful worship service at Trinity as well as all the family involved one way or another. After a honeymoon on Maui, a wedding gift from Dick and Irma Gerlach, Trinity members and friends, they flew off to Princeton, New Jersey where Chris finished his last year at Princeton Seminary before seeking a pastorate.

. . . .

While there, Karen was able to find a teaching job in a wonderful school for the year.

The day after the wedding, August 11, we were presented with gold pins for forty years of service with Wycliffe. It was special to have most of the family there and Greg preach at both Sunday morning services at Trinity.

It was clear that 1997 was a busy year for us, so busy we only put out one newsletter at Christmas. Hugh was covering the years 1934-46 in the life of William Cameron Townsend in his third book on Wycliffe's founder. He was an elder and part of a book club at Trinity along with being involved in choosing committees to serve in seeking a new pastor after George Munzing, Trinity's pastor for 37 ½ years, retired.

I too was probably over-involved with correspondence, prayer groups, grandchildren, editing, writing Bible studies, continuing to lead a weekly Bible study for Trinity's seniors and doing some writing on the side.

While we were heavily involved in church activities, Greg and Wendy were in a position where they were not. At Easter Greg resigned from Naperville Covenant Church over ministry differences. It was a time of uncertainty but God opened an opportunity for Greg to work with David Mains of "Chapel of the Air Ministries," and he enjoyed writing and traveling to promote the 50-day Spiritual Adventure Series.

Lee was in his final year at the University of Virginia. And Karen and Chris gave us the good news that Chris had accepted a call to Trinity Presbyterian Church in Satellite Beach, Florida as Associate Pastor. They found a duplex to rent in Melbourne, about fifteen or twenty minutes away. Karen began teaching 4th grade at a school only minutes away from where they lived. And she was able to keep up her musical talents by singing in a 125-voice community chorus and play her flute in the Bravard Symphony.

We were able to go back to Virginia in June 1998 to see Lee receive his Juris Doctor degree, plus the Eppa Hunton IV Memorial Book Award given to the graduate "who demonstrated unusual aptitude in courses in the field of litigation and who showed a keen awareness and understanding of the lawyer's ethical and professional responsibility." He also was one of six in the graduating class of 380 students who had received a Hardy Cross Dillard Scholarship given to "exceptional members of the entering class based on prior academic achievement, leadership, integrity, service to others, success in endeavors outside the classroom and maturity." We were thrilled and praised God! And we quickly told Paula she should receive a medal, too, for surviving the past three years with the care of three little ones while Lee studied long and hard!

We're not sure which was more exciting—Lee's graduation or him faxing, a mere ten minutes before the graduation ceremony, the final signed papers for the purchase of their first house on ten acres in Fredericksburg, Virginia. And to top off that exciting day, after the graduation ceremony, he went home and taught Walker to ride a two-wheeled bike!

A writer often doesn't hear back what readers think about his or her book or how a life may have been impacted by it. However, Hugh had the joy of hearing that his book *Manuel*, written thirty years previously, was having a great impact in Iceland with Christians who often have to stand alone in their faith. And his book, *They Dared to be Different,* was becoming "an effective tool in Indonesia," wrote one missionary who bought 400 copies to distribute to new Christians, "to teach how a complete change is essential to godly living." At the same time Hugh heard from the Baptist Press in Indonesia that they were going to translate *They Dared to be Different* into Balinese as they felt it was an effective tool for evangelism. We were greatly encouraged by these reports.

In October 1998, Hugh, now sixty-seven, who had been a foster child and finally adopted by Mable and Dave Steven when he was twenty years old, finally met his biological half-sisters and would later meet his half-brother. Unfortunately his biological mother had died four years previously and he never met her. The family knew nothing of Hugh, but they graciously accepted him

and even told me they were sure their mother would have liked me. The way this came about was that Canada finally opened their adoption files to the public and Hugh was able to send for his adoption papers. His father's name was blacked out on the form but Hugh had learned

Hugh and his mother in a photo touched up by Greg!

his last name was Toderas just before we were to be

married. This gave him something to go on and we are grateful to Greg who made the first phone calls and set up a date for us to meet his sisters.

It was unreal how much Hugh looked like his older sister. In fact, the family was sure they all had the same father, but we'll never know. They knew nothing of their mother having another child. It was wonderful for Hugh to receive photos of his mother and see how much he looked like her. And he discovered she liked opera as Hugh does. Uncanny as it might seem, her favorite aria from Madame Butterfly, "One Fine Day," was Hugh's favorite, too! You can learn more from Hugh's memoir, *Finding God in the Shadows.*

At the end of 1998, Hugh was working on the fourth volume on Wycliffe's founder while the third volume had been given a publication date of "Spring 1999." And I was still giving a weekly Bible study to Trinity's seniors. I had just finished one on angels and was beginning a new series in Hebrews. I would go on to teach on the Apostles' Creed, but unexpectedly I would not get to finish the series and this would be the end of my three-year "assignment" that had challenged me as well as given me great joy!

17

Stroke, Heartache, 50th Wedding Anniversary

December 1998 was busy with fifty guests in thirty days. In January 1999, Hugh had a call from Mexico City from Liz Isais, who, along with her husband Juan, were longtime missionaries with Latin America Mission. She had recently read Hugh's books— *Manuel* and *They Dared to be Different*—and thought since Mexico lacked good Christian literature, perhaps Hugh could help in that area. She arranged for him to hold a writer's seminar for about 30 or 40 people March 29-31 in a seminary in Mexico City. Hugh was always happy to share what he had learned from his long years of writing.

After he gave the seminar, I wrote in an April 1999 newsletter we began calling "Steven Update," that his seminar was successful and they invited him back for next year. Medical doctors and schoolteachers attended, along with pastors, communication students and others interested in writing biographies. Hugh was also able to get out to Tasquillo, where we had spent several summers learning the Otomi language in order to get our Mexico resident papers. It was a special joy for him to visit with Raul and Macaria, our Otomi language helpers, and he was able to take many photos in and around that area for Wycliffe's photo files.

. . . .

I also wrote about a new computer Wycliffe gave us to replace Hugh's old one that was painfully slow and outdated. I ended up taking it over as I learned how to do our newsletter and improve my skills in card making. Hugh willingly kept using his old computer and eventually we were able to replace it. Hugh was working on a writing manual from material he had used for his workshops and was hoping to get it published. At the same time he was beginning to work on the fourth volume on the life and times of William Cameron Townsend.

The other news was a trip in June to Canada for Karen, Chris, Dave and Wendy to meet Hugh's birth relatives. It was Chris's first trip to Canada and they were able to come up a week early to join us for a week at Thetis Island and a day hike on the Juan de Fuca trail on Vancouver Island with my sister Shirley joining us. Then on the weekend of June 12-14, Dave and Wendy joined us as we introduced them to Hugh's two sisters and we met Hugh's brother for the first time. It was a lovely reception and I was happy we could meet more of their families and they could meet more of ours.

In this same letter I asked prayer for Wycliffe U.S.A's move to Orlando in July. In that some were not going to move with the office, I asked special prayer for replacements. I was hoping we could move as the new headquarters would be only about an hour from Karen and Chris in Melbourne, but with our wonderful offices here over our garage, it seemed best to stay put. Hugh did miss his weekly visits to interact with his supervisor and other colleagues, but with e-mail, that was not a problem.

In September 1999, I wrote another "Steven Update" to announce Hugh's third book on William Cameron

. . . .

Townsend, *Doorway to the World, the Mexico Years, 1935-47*, would eventually come out in October. It dealt with the beginnings of Wycliffe's work in Mexico that had led to the opening of more than 70 countries with personnel from 46 different countries working in more than 1500 language projects.

I also mentioned Hugh was able to have the reports, letters and diaries from which to tell the Wycliffe story because this information was held in the archive department at the Jungle Aviation and Radio Service headquarters in Waxhaw, North Carolina. Cal Hibbard, Uncle Cam's former secretary, and a team of helpers had worked for more than ten years to archive this material and thus make it available to Hugh and other researchers. Hugh had approximately 25,000 documents from the archives to go through for his next book. In fact, Grandsons Andrew and Jonathan helped to sort the documents by months and years. It was a tedious task but they were happy to have this summer project and earn a bit of pin money as well. Needless to say we were most grateful for the invaluable work Cal and his teammates had done to preserve this history.

There was no way of knowing what would happen next on life's road. I was supposed to have gone to the doctor's for my yearly checkup in July, but we had so much company in July and August, I couldn't get away. I knew I should go, but I just got too busy.

It was a Saturday morning, September 24, 1999. Our usual day for cleaning was on Friday, but Thursday and Friday I had been proof reading the galleys of Hugh's third book on Uncle Cam. I had told Hugh often during the last few years that I thought the editing and proof reading jobs for his books were getting too hard for me. I didn't feel I was doing as good a job as I used to and he needed to find someone else. But this was a rush job and it had to be in the mail by Saturday as the printers wanted it by Monday. I worked around the clock, terribly stressed, all the while feeling inadequate for the job.

I woke up Saturday morning feeling, for lack of a better word, "puny." I told Hugh I just couldn't do the cleaning that day. It would have to wait. He insisted on doing it anyway and said I should just rest. But I couldn't rest as I saw him bustling around doing it all, so I got up to help him. After we were done, Hugh went upstairs to check his email and I went outside for the last job—sweeping off the front porch. As I was out there, the usual heavy traffic noises all of a sudden seemed to be far away and a prickly sensation started in the fingers of my left hand. My left cheek started to feel numb and not knowing what was going on, I came in and laid down on the sofa. When the prickly pins and needles started in my leg, I got up and called my doctor. He was off for the weekend and I was given the number of another doctor, but I didn't feel like calling a new doctor and went back to the sofa to lie down.

At that point, Hugh came down from his office and when he saw me lying on the sofa and looked at me, he knew something was terribly wrong. I explained my symptoms and he immediately gave me two aspirins (the doctor said later that probably saved my life, or at least from paralysis). He called the new doctor who told us to proceed immediately to Emergency. Fortunately Western Medical Hospital is only a few minutes away, but by the time we were walking into Emergency, my left leg was losing its strength.

As we sat in Emergency, it was evident I was having a stroke and fading fast. Hugh had to tell the receptionist twice that I needed treatment right there and then, and finally they took me into one of the curtained emergency rooms. "Triage! Triage!" I heard as I was fitted with tubes and questioned about raising my arms and legs.

Hard as I tried, I couldn't lift my left leg. It was paralyzed. Over the next two hours again and again they asked me questions and in the beginning I slurred my answers, but eventually I could speak clearly and even raise my leg. I praise God for His mercy.

I was transferred to a room where I was observed and kept for two days. The diagnosis was a mild stroke. My leg continued to strengthen but I was so weak it took me weeks to be able to walk any distance. I was 68, but I felt more like 92! Two days before I had taken hour-long walks. Now I couldn't even walk a half block. And for a long time I would veer to the left, walking off the sidewalk! I'm glad that eventually stopped. Like hepatitis, however, it took me two years to get back to where I was before I had the stroke.

I don't think anywhere I've talked about how I love to read, and while most of my reading is theology or devotional, I do like to read a good novel every now and then and I was grateful for all the good books in our church library I could read while recuperating.

With a history of stroke in my family (my mother and father both had strokes) I should have been more careful about checking my blood pressure, but up until that time, I had no problems. You can be sure I'm more diligent now and, of course, I'm on blood pressure pills and blood thinners, and will be, the doctor says, for the rest of my life.

In a letter dated October 27, 1999, I shared what had happened to me. I said I was still having some "residuals" or TIA's (Transient Ischemic Attacks) down the left side of my face, arm and leg. I also said that Hugh had been a wonderful caregiver and the many who brought in meals and other goodies lightened his load considerably. I ended the letter sharing the good news that we finally had received copies of Hugh's third book (the one I proofread that stressed me out!) on Uncle Cam and we were happy with the results.

As soon as I was able, I was back involved in scheduling pray-ers for Sunday morning services, working in Trinity's Samaritan Care Center sending out cards and calling Trinity's homebound, the ill, cancer patients and church members with various health concerns. I began to make cards for the Samaritan Care Center along with another Trinity member. After several years working in the Samaritan Care Center, I resigned but offered to continue to make the cards.

Never to sit around, I took a digital photo imaging course at the senior center, got involved in an early morning prayer meeting and in a ladies' Bible Study, entertained, traveled to see our families, wrote and published articles and poems and, along with our huge correspondence, generally stayed out of mischief!

On February 2, 2000 William Cameron Romig arrived. Need I tell you we loved the name? William was Joan Romig's (Chris's mother) first grandchild and our tenth. We flew to Florida on February 5 and while I helped with household chores and holding William at every opportunity, Hugh worked every day in the Wycliffe office in Orlando (a scant hour north) on their photo files. Karen was able to substitute teach right up until the last week before William arrived and was taking a breather until the fall to see whether she would go back to teach or not. She however, continued to teach flute students and tutor another student in math. Chris was enjoying his pastoral work and praising God that the church was growing with two Sunday morning services and a Saturday evening service.

In August, Hugh finally got a new computer, and William was six months old. He seemed to be crying less, and Karen felt she needed to get back to teaching to help with finances. She went back to her 4th grade class part-time.

In November, the family began to talk about the possibility of having a family reunion for our 50th wedding anniversary on May 5, 2001. The times our family could all get together were becoming more difficult so when the children wanted to know whether we wanted a big party or a reunion for our 50th, we chose the latter. The children had given us a lovely reception in 1976 for our 25th wedding anniversary complete with a three tier wedding cake and many well-wishers who came to the home of our friends, Anne and Mike Wakefield who had opened their home for the celebration.

It had now been a year since my stroke. I was feeling fine but my left leg was still weak and I could no longer do Hugh's editing. The CAT scan had shown some gray cell damage and I felt I was still not thinking or speaking as clearly as before. We were grateful when friends stepped up to help us. Jim Wylie, longtime Trinity friend, and Al Farson, an old friend from Mexico, were happy to help out with the editing and it was a great relief for Hugh, and me!

Fifty years. Our Golden Wedding Anniversary. We were 70 years old and had been in Wycliffe 45 years. Time to celebrate to be sure! We couldn't believe how much living had taken place in these years.

There were twenty-one of us who congregated in Seaside, Oregon in a newly decorated former bed and breakfast seven-bedroom, eight-bathroom house that Wendy had found on line. Why Seaside? It's where we had our honeymoon and we hadn't been back.

We were a block from the beach. We played in the sand, flew kites and took side trips to Astoria, Cannon Beach and Tillamook. The older grandchildren played Pit until the wee hours of the morning. The younger ones went to a butterfly farm and a carousel in town, and William enjoyed the aquarium and a child-sized train ride.

One day we thought it would be fun to look for the North Prom Hotel where we had stayed for our honeymoon. Every family needs a Greg Asimakoupoulos! He checked around and found the original building had burned to the ground except for one small section. It turned out to be just around the corner from where we were! And he not only found this for us, but he went to Seaside's Chamber of Commerce and told them of our return to Seaside after fifty years and they donated special bags with souvenirs, one for each of us. He even contacted a reporter to interview us and take our photo for an article that came out on the front page of the local paper.

It was a toss-up whether the best part of our week was early morning together over cups of coffee, or the discussions that came out of an assignment Hugh gave us all to read C.S. Lewis's, *The Last Battle*. We were to look for themes of death and heaven that we could discuss around the table after mealtimes. There was lively banter and differences of opinion at times, but all in good humor. David Jr., who had brought along his girlfriend Heather Sielaff said, "I hope when we get married we will have discussions like this around our table."

The Steven clan in front of the "Fort Stevens State Park" marker, near Seaside, Oregon. Greg took the photo

In writing to our many friends about our 50th wedding anniversary celebration, I thought I'd like to let them know what I'd learned in fifty years of marriage and enclosed the following in my letters:

1. Two are better than one.

2. If I trust God with all my heart and put Him first, my world will not fall apart if my husband disappoints me.

3. To always keep the lines of communication open and talk over problems but choose the timing. It might be better to "sleep on it."

4. It's important not to let the "sun go down on my anger," but seek God's help to forgive my husband and others—even if I have to be the first to say, "I'm sorry"—every time.

5. Forgiveness does not come naturally. I need to work at it right along with love.

6. To live with eternity in view. My mother's comment, "It's all for the burning" (when Christ returns) has helped me gain a right perspective on material loss and unfulfilled dreams and desires.

7. That meeting God at the beginning of each day for prayer, reflection, worship, reading and the study of God's Word, quiets my spirit, strengthens and equips me for what I may encounter that day. It gives balance, sets priorities, fills me with His peace, joy and presence, and helps me think God's thoughts after Him.

8. God alone satisfies. Things don't.

9. Materialism is a snare. The churning for more, better, bigger or newer never stops. Therefore, I need to learn to be content with what I have.

10. Godliness (a good and holy life with deep reverence for God) with contentment is indeed great gain (1 Timothy 6:6).

11. God has fashioned me for joy and a joyful spirit is more attractive than a face-lift.

12. The grass is not always greener on the other side. What God gives is for my good.

13. A sense of humor and not taking myself too seriously is an asset.

14. Waiting for God to reveal His will is difficult, but best.

15. To remember that "this too shall pass" when faced with financial, health, marital or family problems. God is worthy to be trusted and nothing can separate me from His love (Romans 8:35).

16. God makes himself responsible for me.

17. I must will to love my husband if my love has grown cold and seek God's help to demonstrate my love "'til death do us part."

18. Marriage is not a 50/50 proposition but 100% for me, even if my husband is not giving his share.

19. It pleases God when I learn to deny myself and not demand my rights, but mutual submission will make it easier.

20. It is far better to give than get.

21. To allow others to be their own persons. No two are alike.

22. It's okay to agree to disagree. My opinion isn't necessarily always right.

23. To worry less and trust more is a worthy goal.

24. To be more flexible, love unconditionally and serve each other in love makes life more palatable.

25. It's important, with God's help, to work at putting off jealousy, anger, manipulation, grumbling, hurt feelings, negativeness, complaining, criticism, envy, covetousness, comparison, discontentment, judging others, sloth and other things too numerous to mention that I'm still having to "put off."

26. I need to live an examined life before God and deal daily with my revealed sin and weaknesses instead of dwelling on my husband's faults and shortcomings.

27. I need to tell my husband I love him every day.

28. We need to greet each other when we come in, and say "good-bye" when we leave.

20. To kiss my husband often.

30. To let my husband know he's important by giving him a special celebration for his birthday.

31. To bring home an unexpected gift or treat now and then.

32. That a clean, orderly home and good meals make my husband happy.

33. To go out on a date (even to MacDonald's) as often as possible.

34. Vacations or just getting away overnight or for a weekend are important.

35. Take time to enjoy each other and take an interest in what each other is doing.

36. Pray together. Weep together. Rejoice together.

37. Reading a good book while listening to good music with my husband is as enjoyable as going out for an expensive dinner—maybe better!

38. Becoming a good listener is as important as being a good conversationalist.

39. A man enjoys compliments just as much as a woman.

40. It's good to remember my vows. That way divorce is not an option.

41. Children are indeed a reward from God (Psalm 17:30) and worth all the effort it takes to bring them up to follow Him wholeheartedly and take Him seriously.

42. Having my own space is necessary now and then, especially while rearing children.

43. Good friends are treasures, not to be easily let go.

44. Encouragement has greater value than correction.

45. It's important to allow for growth in my husband, others and me.

46. Nagging tears down. Affirmation builds.

47. Tolerance and long-suffering are virtues.

48. Dishonesty destroys. Honesty IS the best policy.

49. God honors risk takers.

50. I want to continue to grow, learn and become all God planned for me to be.

As we looked back over fifty years of marriage and 45 years in Wycliffe and how God had taken us through highs and lows, sickness and health, plenty and want and blessings too numerous to mention, our hearts were full of thanksgiving for God's bountiful goodness to us. We looked ahead, too, knowing we wanted to finish well and continue to do all for the display of His splendor however many years He had allotted to us.

18

Terrorists, Sadness, Haida Wedding

The year 2001 began with the joy of our 50th wedding anniversary. Now however, we cannot think of 2001 without thinking "terrorists." While we were not affected by this diabolical act with the loss of a loved one, we nevertheless grieved for the loss of so many. We had our own grief the month before on August 13, when Jinx Robbins, our daughter-in-law Kristi's mother, was killed in a tragic car accident when she was on her way to church. I remember saying to Dave when he called in tears, "Don't tell me that." A strange response, but I just couldn't put it into my grid. How hard for them all. She was so alive, beautiful and vibrant, still teaching school and active at Trinity.

In October, Hugh had two successful lens implants five weeks apart. All he paid was a co-pay of $10.00. We were glad we were with Kaiser Permanente! Because Hugh had these implants, he was unable to attend the November 25 dedication of the complete Chamula Bible. But we rejoiced in this continuing remarkable story of the entrance of the gospel into this southern Mexico area where there were now numerous chapels and thousands of Christians meeting regularly to study God's Word in their own language. Hugh recorded this in his book, *They Dared to be*

. . . .

Different, and while he would have loved to have been there, as he was for the New Testament dedication, it was nice to hear that *They Dared to be Different* would soon be out in an Italian edition.

Christmas 2001 we flew to Florida where we had Christmas with Karen, Chris and William. Wendy, Greg and the girls joined us for a few days after Christmas.

In our Christmas letter, I asked prayer for Hugh as he finished the fourth volume on William Cameron Townsend, for our travel safety, Lee's daily train travel in to Washington, D.C., and for our nations' leaders to have wisdom in apprehending the terrorists so that we could "live peaceful and quiet lives in all godliness and holiness" (1 Timothy 2:3).

In 2002 we had earned enough free miles to fly to Chicago to spend Easter with Wendy and Greg and family and then fly to Nova Scotia to visit our friends, Jocelyn and Wayne Cameron. We enjoyed seeing the Camerons again and the quaintness of small fishing villages all around them. One disappointment was not being able to see Anne of Green Gables' home on Prince Edward Island as it was not yet open for the tourist season.

One memorable excursion in Halifax was to Pier 21, a Canadian Immigration Museum, and site of the hundreds of thousands of immigrants who landed on Canadian shores from 1928-1971. We had hoped to see my grandparents' names, but since the Ottos came to Canada in 1903 and the Van Boeyens in 1909, there was no available record. Apparently they came in at Pier 2 that was destroyed in 1917 in a munitions ship explosion in Halifax harbor. This huge explosion also destroyed half the city.

Our visit coincided with the death of the Queen Mother and a special place in the museum was cordoned off with a *Book of Remembrance* where anyone could give their condolences and sign their name. I did! Interestingly, after leaving Canada in 1970 and receiving my U.S. citizenship in 1999, after all these years, I still feel a tug toward Royalty and my Canadian roots.

In November 2002, we flew back to Chicago to have Thanksgiving with Wendy and Greg. We were also able to visit with Jonathan as he was studying world religions at Wheaton College. One evening we went over to see how he had fixed up his room and coming down the icy steps of his apartment...you guessed it—I fell! This resulted in a huge hematoma on my knee that eventually dissipated, but it was just one of my many falls over the years.

It was with great sadness we learned, in February 2003, that my sister Eileen's husband, Norman McCurrie, had an inoperable brain tumor and had lost his ability to speak clearly. He had been Hugh's Best Man and had always had a special place in our hearts. He was a wonderful storyteller and always had a joke to make us laugh. We loved to visit them in their lovely home on thirty acres in Coombs, B.C. and we knew this beloved husband and father's loss would be difficult for the family. It was a hard death and I was grateful I could be with Eileen through this difficult time. As Hugh said, "Seeing Norman in such deep distress was sobering and made me realize life's brevity." We still remember the plaintive strains of "Amazing Grace" played by a bagpiper at the graveside where Hugh gave the closing prayer.

. . . .

October 2003 was a milestone for Chris, Karen's husband, who received a call to be senior pastor for Venice Presbyterian Church on the west coast of Florida just below Sarasota. And it was a good move for Karen who joined the Venice Symphony Orchestra and also has many opportunities to play her flute.

Chris's installation service was in February 2004. We were able to attend and then drive up to Virginia for a few days with Lee, Paula, Walker, Isabel and Marshall. On the way we stopped overnight with Billy and Patty Gibson on St. Simons Island, Georgia. We had known them over the years when he was on the Board of Wycliffe Associates and they had invited us often to visit them. It was also interesting to see the famous tree where John and Charles Wesley had prayed before they began their ministry in America.

Over the years I've had very little time with my sisters, so when Brenda, Eileen's daughter, wrote in March 2004 to invite Shirley and I along with her mom and sister Cathie and herself to spend a weekend at a refurbished hotel in Victoria, I jumped at the chance. Brenda is an accountant with a hotel chain and is often offered free rooms at new hotels to check them out. It was an absolutely delightful weekend, a rare opportunity to all be together.

In May 2004, I received a Mother's Day card from Karen and she signed it, "Karen, Chris, William and ?" I let out my usual scream and called her immediately. Yes, indeed, she was pregnant! We rejoiced that William would have a brother.

With a large family, it always seems someone is going or coming, and 2004 was no different. Allison, Wendy and

Greg's middle daughter, graduated from high school and in August left for a year to attend the Covenant Bible College in Quito, Ecuador. Jonathan, Dave & Kristi's middle son, was back at Wheaton College. Kristin was back for her Junior year at Hope College in Holland, Michigan and had been on staff at Mt. Hermon Christian Camp and Conference Center all summer. In October, Hugh and I visited Wendy, Greg and Lauren and took a side trip to Holland, Michigan to see Kristin in her college environment and as a participant in "The Pull," a huge, and I mean HUGE, tug-of-war contest for which Hope College is famous. As soon as we got home, we drove to Tucson, Arizona for an Otto cousin reunion. I met seven of my first cousins I had never met before! And, of course, we had to make a trip to Florida in November to see our 11th grandchild, Nicholas Steven Romig, born October 29, 2004.

There is one more trip I need to mention. My sister Shirley and I flew up to the Queen Charlotte Islands (now called Haida Gwaii) in B.C., Canada to attend the traditional Haida wedding of our grandniece, Nika, my sister Mabel's granddaughter. We stayed in little hotel that was in the street-level basement of a house called "Gracie's Place" in Queen Charlotte City, and on the day of the wedding, we drove to the village of Skidegate where my sister had lived for forty years. It was fun to see her lovely three-story home that faced the ocean.

When it was time, we stood on the beach with hundreds of other guests (the whole village had been invited to the wedding, plus other guests). Then around a corner from another small island in the bay came a canoe with the bride, Nika Brown, my grandniece, in a beautiful long white cape with Haida designs, wearing the native conical straw hat. As the canoe pulled up to the shores, the paddlers raised their oars, Nika was helped out of the canoe onto the beach where she stood with her mother Amanda and between them her *Nanai* (my sister Mabel and Nika's grandmother) to await the groom who was coming in another canoe.

And then the groom, Danny Robertson, grandson of H.R. MacMillan, Canadian lumber entrepreneur and adventurer, in a kilt and formal jacket, shirt and black bow tie, appeared standing in a ceremonial hand-carved canoe, filled with paddlers.

He called out to the village chief for permission to come on land, and the chief, in full Haida regalia, welcomed him. Danny climbed out of the canoe and came ashore while drummers and dancers celebrated. And then we all proceeded up the hill to the Community Hall with the bride and groom in front and all the guests trailing behind them.

There were tables and chairs set up for everyone with new dishes, bowls, mugs and silverware that the guests were to take with them when they left. I lost track of the number of fish dishes we had. The women of the village had cooked all week and had a refrigerated container where they had stored everything. Shirley and I were invited to sit at the main table with the other relatives. Sister Mabel was only there a short time as she wasn't

feeling too well. There were native dancers and speeches and much celebrating with cheers and clapping.

On Sunday, Shirley and I went to the United Church in Skidegate. When a woman came and sat beside me, to my happy surprise I discovered she was Mabel's sister-in-law, Thelma.

To say our time in Haida Gwaii was delightful is an understatement. It was an experience of a lifetime. How rich I am for having these relatives in our family tree.

There was good news in the area of Hugh's books. *Yours to Finish the Task,* the fourth volume on the life and times of William Cameron Townsend, was finally in hand in a handsome volume. We were also pleased that Elizabeth Işias, for whom Hugh had held a writer's workshop in Mexico City, had translated *Manuel* and *Manuel, the Continuing Story* and published them in Spanish in one volume. And *They Dared to be Different* had also come out in a Spanish edition.

Hugh had been working on a book about writing gleaned from his many years of experience and finally in 2005 he self published it under the title, *The Nature of Story and Creativity.* He was also becoming a mentor and Wycliffe historian for several writers in Wycliffe needing historical data on the beginnings of Wycliffe. And we continued our trips to see our children—two to Mercer Island, Washington where Greg had accepted a call as Senior Pastor of Mercer Island Covenant Church. It was hard to leave the mid-west they had grown to love, and a hard adjustment for Lauren in high school, but God was calling Greg back into the pastorate and this was an open door for him. For us we were thrilled as we could now drive to see them on the west coast! We were looking forward to their coming the end of December. Lauren and her school band were scheduled to play and march in the Rose Parade, January 2, 2006.

Like grandparents, like grandchildren, I guess, because they were traveling, too, but a much farther distance. Andrew, Dave & Kristi's youngest son, was in Quito, Ecuador at the same Bible School Allison attended the previous year, and Kristin would be going out in January with International Teams Youth World to work with teens in Quito for five months. To top off our globe-trotting grandchildren, Jonathan was in Limerick, Ireland for a year to play basketball with a professional team.

In February 2006, I felt a nudge to read to Maggie Weatherstone, a homebound friend. Like asking my arthritic friend, Esther Palmer, if I could put lotion on her legs since she could no longer bend down, I wondered at first if this is what God wanted me to do. Again I was fearful of asking her, but I put caution to the wind, and she was delighted. Maggie had been in a wheelchair long before she and her husband Joe came to Trinity. She was a great editor and had done some good editing for us. I knew she had been an avid reader, but now she had blurred vision due to a fall she had on a trip to Mexico and could no longer read.

I visited her from time to time and when she told me she hadn't been able to finish the last book of the Mitford Series, *Light from Heaven*, I asked her if she'd like me to read it to her. So we began, week by week and we finished it in July. She also loved poetry so I would read her Darlene Bee's poems from her book, *Earthen Vessels*. Darlene, a former Wycliffe member, wrote sensitive poems that dealt with her own emotional struggles, and often the words were helpful to Maggie.

I believe it was as good a time for her as it was for me. Over the months, however, she was getting weaker and thinner. We would be traveling for the summer, but I told her to think about what book we could read for the fall. In the fall, however, she was not too well and she passed away in November. I am so happy we had that time together and it brings me pleasure to think of Maggie running free in heaven with good eyesight!

It was also in February 2006 that Hugh began to have breathing problems and pains in his right shoulder and down his right side. I wanted to call 911, but Hugh said, "No!" So I called the Kaiser Permanent nurse and she said he should go to the Urgicenter in Costa Mesa. However I couldn't get him out of the sofa. It was too painful. And I was nervous about driving him on the freeway as it was a distance away and there was a rain storm on the way.

I was praying silently, asking God to help me know what to do when the phone rang. It was Peggy Blaising, a friend from Trinity and King's Class, and she started by asking how I was. She knew I had just gotten over the flu so I told her I was still weak but what was more of a concern was Hugh's situation. She immediately said, "Hold it! Jim and I are coming. We'll take you." My response was, "Jesus loves me this I know!" They helped me get Hugh into their car and they drove us to the Urgicenter and stayed with us. Since it was going to take a long time until Hugh was ready to leave, he insisted that we leave. It turned out Hugh was there six and a half hours! The torrential rain storm hit when he was on his way home in a taxi. I was so grateful I didn't have to drive in it and praised God for sensitive, helpful friends!

The x-ray showed a large mass in the lower right lobe of his lung. The diagnosis was pneumonia. To get any sleep at all he had to sit upright. He was scheduled to teach a course on writing at Trinity, but had to cancel.

In the middle of March, Hugh was still not feeling well and went back to see his doctor. The news was not good. His pneumonia was now in both lungs and he was put on a new antibiotic for two weeks. We were concerned as we were set to leave at the end of March to fly to Wycliffe's Headquarters in Dallas where Hugh was to be recognized for the body of work he had produced through his some thirty Wycliffe books. Fortunately in two days he turned a corner. His voice was stronger and his coughing less and we thanked God for His healing.

The person who spearheaded this special recognition was Wycliffe member, Carol Chaney. We were with Bob and Carol Chaney during our 10 ½ years in Mexico but had not had that much contact with them since leaving Mexico some thirty-eight years ago. It was a lovely surprise she did this for Hugh and on April 1st we left for SIL's International Headquarters in Dallas. Kirby O'Brien, son of our dear friends Danny and Bev O'Brien and now, with his wife Jackie, Wycliffe members, had painted a portrait of Uncle Cam that would be unveiled at the special museum event where Hugh would be featured with his books.

We stayed in the Cowan Apartments that have been built as senior housing for retired Wycliffe missionaries. They were wonderful—spacious and adequate. We were delighted to see so many of our Mexico Branch Wycliffe friends.   About seventy people had gathered, Kirby's painting was unveiled and Hugh was at a table with all his books, including the 4th book on Uncle Cam, *Yours to Finish the Task.* He was happy he sold quite a few!

In the evening we were asked to speak at a special dinner about our family and what we were now doing. It was a lovely time of fellowship and we're so grateful to Carol Chaney for arranging this.

Our plan was to fly on to Tampa and visit with Karen and Chris seeing we had half our way paid, but we had a terrible time getting on our way. We sat on the tarmac from 7:50 a.m. to 11:55 a.m.   They had to replace a computer, and we sat so long, they needed more fuel. As it was the first day of Daylight Saving Time, we heard that the co-pilot forgot to set his clock ahead!   Only one passenger demanded to get off. We arrived in Tampa at 4:00 p.m. hungry and tired but all was erased with big hugs from William and Nicholas.

One of the reasons for going to Tampa at this time was because Karen and Chris were giving a pre-Lenten musical program. Pat and Bruce Higgins, a newly-wed couple we had met in Mexico, were now retired and living about twenty minutes away in Sarasota. It was wonderful to have them share the program with us.

On May 5, 2006, we celebrated fifty-five years of marriage. Time for another celebration! This time we chose Port Ludlow, Washington as someone in Wendy and Greg's church had waterfront property and they offered us two side-by-side condos free of charge. All of us were able to be together for a week, except for Andrew who could only come for a couple of days. The highlight of that week was Greg baptizing grandchildren Jonathan, 24, Allison, 20 and Lauren, 16, in the cold ocean. What a blessing to hear them confess they wanted to follow Jesus, "all their lives." Afterwards Chris prayed a special blessing over each of the eleven grandchildren. A little bit of heaven to be sure!

Hugh continued to interact with more writers—ten in all—mentoring, editing or helping with Wycliffe historical data. Many of our friends were at the age when they were

55th Wedding Anniversary, Port Ludlow, WA, May 5, 2006 (actually celebrated in June). L. to R. by family: Lee, Paula, Isabel, Walker, Marshall (kneeling). Greg, Wendy, Allison, Lauren, Kristin (kneeling). Norma, Hugh. Karen, Chris, Nicholas, William (standing).Kristi, Dave, Heather, Dave, Jonathan

....

writing their memoirs and Hugh was helping several with their projects as well.

As for the grandchildren, they were continuing their adventures. Jonathan finished his season playing pro basketball in Ireland and went to China with a team of  Christian athletes to play basketball for three weeks before flying to Poland to play pro basketball. Son Lee, an international lawyer, traveled to Turkey for two weeks. Andrew finished his second semester at the Covenant Bible School in Quito, Ecuador and Kristin was back from Quito as well and now at University Presbyterian Church in Seattle where she was an intern working with high school girls.

Before I get farther along with my remembrances, I need to mention that Lauren was becoming a fine flutist, winning awards all over the place. At the end of 2006 she had won a national wind ensemble competition to play with others from across the nation in Carnegie Hall in New York in May 2007. Wendy and Greg would go along and celebrate their 25th anniversary as well. Other awards she accrued were written up on her brochure when she gave a Senior (High School) flute recital on April 26, 2009. She wrote:

> I have participated in Seattle's Junior Youth Symphony Orchestra, Northwest High Schools Honor Band, All-State Band and All-Northwest Orchestra. I am a regional Solo and Ensemble competition winner and last year placed first in flute in Washington State's Solo and Ensemble

competition. I have competed in Seattle Flute
Society's Horsfall competition and this year
received an Honorable Mention. I have
participated and received superior ratings in Seattle
Young Artists Music Festival and Performing Arts
Festival of the Eastside.

She also listed several flutists with whom she had the
privilege of participating in Master classes. Pretty
impressive for an 18-year-old!

Not to be outdone, Karen was going to be the featured
flute soloist in February with the Venice (Florida)
Symphony Orchestra. Along with these achievements
congratulations were due Kristi who went back for her 5th
year of college to earn her teacher's credential.

In February 2007, we flew back to hear Karen as the
guest flutist for the Venice Symphony Orchestra and we
were happy Karen and Chris were having many
opportunities to give concerts together.

In June we flew back to Fredericksburg, Virginia to
enjoy a week with Lee, Paula and the family on their
beautiful acreage. An added joy was Karen, Chris and
their two boys flying up for a few days and we had a
delightful time watching William and Nicholas interact
with their cousins.

Then we had visits with my older sister Eileen and her
two daughters, Cathie and Brenda and later with Shirley,
my younger sister and we drove over to Tucson for
another mini-reunion with a few of our Otto cousins and
our last remaining aunt, Auntie Addie.

Hugh continued to mentor several writers and we had
the joy of looking forward to our first great grandchild,

due in February. This would be David Jr. and Heather's first child and the first grandchild on both sides of their families.

In the fall I began teaching English as a Second Language (ESL) in our church's English Center and looked forward to it every week.   Most were Japanese and Korean women, though I did have one Mexican woman, as well as a Peruvian.

Christmas was coming and Wendy, Greg and the girls would be arriving Christmas morning. No, there were no exotic trips in 2007 that many in their retirement make, but, for us, the joy of seeing family was better than any trip to a faraway place, and we relished each and every visit.

19

ESL, Great Grandson, God's Assignments

On January 1, 2008, I wrote in my journal: "Open my eyes and mind to discover new truths that I may reach a new understanding of how to live for You and display Your splendor. Deepen my knowledge of You that I may know You better."

Little did I know this prayer would be abundantly answered as I joined with Trinity members to read, in one year, *The Daily Walk Bible* in the New Living Translation. Each day I was blessed. I also began to reread the daily devotional *Streams in the Desert*. Both of these were like year-long manna from heaven!

Mid-January we had our first incident of graffiti on our garage door in red paint. I wanted to move right away, but of course we couldn't. It wasn't a good time to sell the house with the economic downturn, and we didn't know where we'd go! We had two more episodes of graffiti, one the city steam cleaned, but after that we've had no other incidents, for which I am most grateful!

We began to look into getting new windows. One estimate was around $7,000.00, but the company never got back to us with a contract. We finally settled on using the same company Dave and Kristi had used to replace theirs.

The bill was almost $10,000 because we added a new front door and patio sliding door, but we've cut our heating and cooling bills tremendously.

Termites are one of the negatives about living in Southern California. They can really cause havoc. Our garage was showing signs of them feasting on our rafters and we had to call in the termite man to the tune of $500.00. Then we had them in the banister going up to our offices over the garage and in the stoop of the back door entrance and had to take care of that. We also had fierce winds in January 2008. On Grand Avenue, a couple of blocks away, twenty telephone poles were downed. We sustained damage as well. Our awning over the office stairs ripped and had to be replaced. So along with the window expense and termite repair, we praised God for the ability to pay these bills and still remain solvent!

I continued to teach English as a Second Language (ESL) every Tuesday morning from 9:00 to 12:30. One morning, Christine, one of my Korean students, sat down at the piano in our kindergarten Sunday School classroom where our class met, and began to play *God is so Good*. As she began to sing in English, the other students gathered around her and joined in. They sounded great and I decided this would be our assembly program (all classes were urged to give an assembly program. It could be whatever we wanted). Since they were all Christians, we felt this would be a testimony as well to the many non-Christians who attend.

Karen and Chris in Florida were tremendously encouraged when Will's drama teacher wrote a note home that said: "I just wanted to tell you how much I enjoy William in my class. He will always participate and seems to enjoy drama and public speaking. He is sweet, well behaved and very creative. Congratulations on a great son." Oh for more teachers who understand the importance of encouragement!

On February 28, 2008 (Allison's birthday as well!), another Steven milestone was reached. Our first great grandson was born! David Jr. and Heather had a healthy baby boy, Luke  David. What a blessing to see a third generation being brought up to know and love the Lord. We were able to attend his dedication in January.

In early 2008 I heard from my sister Eileen about the possibility of Shirley, Eileen and I going on an Alaska cruise along with Eileen's two daughters, Cathie and Brenda. We were all set for September 1 to September 7. Brenda not only got us a discount fare but also a complimentary hotel room in Vancouver for August 30. Hugh and I would drive up to Vancouver, stay overnight at the hotel, Hugh would drop me off at the ship in the morning and go on over to Vancouver Island to stay in Shirley's condo while we were cruising for a week.

In April, when Wendy was down visiting, we looked for a formal for the one formal dinner during the cruise, and I was so pleased I found one on sale. I was excited and looking forward to my first-ever cruise anywhere.

In the meantime, Eileen went for her annual mammogram. It was negative, but about five weeks later she woke up to pain and when she finally got in to see the doctor, the diagnosis was Inflammatory Breast Cancer. It was a terrible shock, yet she was so positive. She was scheduled for a series of chemotherapy treatments and the doctor felt she would be able to go on the cruise.

After three chemo treatments, however, they discovered they hadn't made a difference. It was soon obvious the cruise was not about to happen. Eileen then went to Victoria for five weeks of radiation five days a week after that surgery.

We cancelled the cruise and in June 2008 Hugh and I had two back-to-back trips: One to Fredericksburg to be with Lee, Paula and the children and also Karen, Chris and the boys flew up from Florida as they had in 2007. With Lee and Paula on ten acres and a huge back yard, it was wonderful to see William and Nicholas running around with their cousins the second year in a row.

We got home and then flew up to Seattle to have a week

Sister trio: Eileen, Shirley, Norma

with Wendy and Greg. During that week Wendy joined us to drive up overnight to Burnaby, a suburb of Vancouver, to attend a Van Boeyen cousin reunion. It was delightful to see my first cousins, Dorothy, Patricia and Marjorie again after so many years, along with some of their children we had never met.

In September I went back to teaching ESL after having the summer off. Hugh put the finishing touches on his book of Herman Aschmann's memoirs and tried to find a publisher.

Once again, Karen and Chris were performing. This time on November 3, 2008 in Venice Presbyterian Church's Community Concert Series. We were disappointed we couldn't go back for it, especially since they played *Clair de Lune* by Claude Debussy, one of Hugh's favorite pieces.

Under Karen's accomplishments in the program, it read, in part:

> Karen Romig began playing the flute at the age of eight. In high school and college Karen continued to develop her artistic abilities under the tutelage of Arthur Hoberman, flutist with the famed 20th Century-Fox studio orchestra. After college she studied with Bonita Boyd, Julius Baker and Anne Giles (principal flutist with the Los Angeles Philharmonic). Karen graduated summa cum laude from Chapman University in Flute Performance. She has won numerous awards including first place in the Sigma Alpha Iota Competition and first place in the Musical Arts Club of Orange County Competition. Karen has played in orchestras in California and Florida and has been a featured soloist at various venues.

Chris, too, had a nice write-up that stated, in part:

> Chris Romig plunged into piano lessons at age seven
> after attending a live performance by Liberace.
> Beginning on a three-octave toy piano, Chris soon
> advanced to an upright piano borrowed from his
> grandparents' home. He began playing frequently at
> his home church in Adelphi, Maryland, and became
> the church organist at 14. During his undergraduate
> study at the University of Maryland, Chris
> performed extensively as a pianist in Washington,
> D.C. area. As a graduate student at Princeton
> Theological Seminary, he served as Associate Chapel
> Organist at the Seminary and Director of Music at
> the Witherspoon Street Presbyterian Church.

Before we knew it, it was Christmas again. Hugh felt we
shouldn't put up a tree as none of the children were going
to be coming home. But I insisted and up went our fake
tree that later Hugh admitted he enjoyed.

I found myself melancholy on Christmas Eve with most
of the family so scattered. We would have Christmas
dinner with Dave & Kristi and their family. We've always
been thankful we've had at least one family close. But
somehow it didn't seem right that the other three families
were going to be alone, too. I sat down and wrote:

Remembering Christmas Eves

There's a joy in remembering,
Mixed with sadness and pain,

There's a hope of reunion when together again.
But the loneliness smothers;
There's more shadow than light,
And I long for my family on this Holy Night.

I remember the stockings, the gifts piled so high,
There was laughter and peeking,
Lots of goodies and pie,
There were cookies for Santa, what a marvelous sight
As my family was near me on this Holy Night.
But now they are gone with their own families,
They're gathering around their own Christmas trees;
And I hear their faint laughter, but find no delight
Without family near me on this Holy Night.

O Savior, sweet Savior,
Turn my thoughts toward You;
Help me to remember You came to renew,
To bring us salvation, to bring us Your light…
I'll remember Your coming on this Holy Night!

This helped me to turn my thoughts once again to the
reason for the Season and get out of my pity party. But I
did miss them!

January 2009 dawned and I was back teaching ESL after
a two-week break. One of my students, Gina, a new
Christian from a Buddhist background, asked if I would
give her private lessons, and while I had enough to do to
keep me busy at my age, I somehow felt I should say
"yes."

In 2002, the editor of "Just Between Us," a magazine for pastor's wives, accepted an article I wrote on forgiveness. I titled my article, "Amateur Forgivers." It basically dealt with what I have already shared in this book--my struggle of many years to forgive my abusive father. Amazingly, the editors of a journal for pastors on mission and theology in Korea picked up my article and reprinted it. Two years later they also used another article I had written and I cherished these journals, even though I couldn't read Korean. It was encouraging to realize that pastors and others were reading my articles in Korea. I prayed they would find them helpful.

Now five years later, I remembered the journals and thought Gina would enjoy knowing her English teacher had published in her home country. I put the journals on the coffee table for her to see. With her limited English and my non-existent Korean, I hoped perhaps the books might open some conversation.

I had a sheet of conversational questions I had retrieved from the Internet, but never got to use them. Immediately after Gina sat down, she saw the journals and began to scan the article on forgiveness.

"Why father angry?" I knew my answer would have to be short for her to grasp understanding. I scrambled to think of a few words that would describe my complex father.

"Bitterness," I said. "He was very bitter."

She got out her electronic dictionary and looked up the word, "bitter." Slowly she nodded her head in understanding.

"Why bitter?" she asked.

Again I knew I couldn't give a full explanation of my dad going through the Great Depression, the hard, dirty work of an oil burner mechanic while his younger brother was his boss, being cheated out of money by so-called Christians, and a religious but unloving father.

"Harsh, " I said simply. "His father was *harsh*."

She looked it up in her dictionary and again nodded and looked pained. Then she turned to me and patting her chest said, "I bitter. I bitter with my sister."

Her story came out in broken sentences but God helped me to piece it together and understand.

"No forgive," she said.

"It's hard," I responded, "but God wants us to forgive." I gestured, patting my hand over my heart. "If we don't forgive, we become bitter, too."

She understood! Tears filled her eyes. Suddenly she said, "I need Bible study. You give me Bible study?"

I told her I would.

As I thought about this incident later that afternoon, I was overwhelmed with how God does indeed, "not waste anything." Sixty years ago my life was miserable at home and I carried scars for years. This caused me to write an article on forgiveness seven years ago that was published in Korea. The article was in a Korean journal, now sitting on my coffee table so that a young Korean woman, who was struggling with an inability to forgive her sister, could read it in Santa Ana, California and realize she needed God's help. Only God could engineer that!

The next day I was at a Bible study and shared this amazing story with the woman I was seated beside. "Oh," she said, "you need to talk with Grace Dowdell. She just told me the other day she was looking for a new ministry."

I knew Grace. I had her in my WOW Bible study years ago. She was a Korean married to a Caucasian.

I called her and she was willing to come and be my interpreter. I had been wondering how I was going to be able to explain spiritual truths when I couldn't speak Korean. I had committed it to the Lord, had asked His help and was trusting Him to help me give His truth to Gina. Once again God knew my need and supplied.

One of the other Korean ESL students overheard Gina talking about the Bible study and asked if she could come, and so we began with the four of us: Gina, Young Mi, Grace and myself. It was obvious Young Mi had been walking with the Lord a long time and was able to explain things to Gina along with Grace. It was a wonderful study. I had made a short outline on verses dealing with forgiveness in the Bible and we read these in English for English practice, and then Young Mi and Gina took turns reading it in their Korean Bibles.

In the next lessons we studied about new life in Christ, submission, prayer, that we are chosen to live for the praise of His Glory and our hope in Christ. Then Grace and her family were going on a two-week vacation and God took me out of the picture as well.

It was Tuesday morning, my regular day for teaching ESL at Trinity. The weather was strange. One minute the sun was out. The next we had a tropical downpour. It did this a couple of times before we had our assembly break at 10:45 a.m. Some places on the sidewalk did not drain well. Others were wet and slimy, and I hit one. My feet went out from under me and with a vengeance I slammed down on my left side on the wet cement.

I knew I had seriously hurt myself because when I tried to move, the pain was intense. Several who were also on their way to the assembly, came running. I didn't see who they were. I was in such pain I kept my eyes tightly closed. Someone cradled my upper body and I found out later it was Shelly Potts on staff in Trinity's Children's department. I had never met her, but she was such a comfort. I wrote her a note of thanks, and when we had a special meeting two and a half months later for the mortgage burning of Trinity's new Fellowship Hall, I met her personally and finally got to give her a hug and big personal thank you.

Trinity's Parish nurse, Nancy Amo, felt an ambulance should be called as they didn't want to move me if I had a broken leg or pelvis. When the ambulance arrived, the paramedics kept asking me my name and if I had hit my head. I assured them I hadn't hit my head and gave my name many times. Finally, they put me on the gurney and off I went, sans siren, with Nancy Amo in the front with the driver and Hugh, who had been called, following in our car. I was admitted to Emergency in Kaiser Permanente Lakeview Hospital in Anaheim Hills and laid there for ten hours because they had no vacant beds!

Around noon I was x-rayed but they said it was "inconclusive". They wheeled me back to my cubbyhole in Emergency and there was son Dave waiting for me. I burst into tears. It was so special of him to come from work to see his old mother. We visited, then they came to take me to get a CAT scan and Dave went back to work. I was grateful the scan showed no broken bones.

I was cleared to be discharged but as I was getting dressed to come home, I passed out. My blood pressure suddenly plunged. They revived me and as I tried to get dressed, I passed out again. I had arrived at 11:30 a.m. and it was now around 5:30 p.m. but there were still no vacant beds, so I stayed in Emergency on the gurney.

I called Kristi around 7:30 p.m. (they live only about ten minutes from the hospital) and asked if she wouldn't mind bringing me a toothbrush and toothpaste, some socks (my feet were freezing), and some pajamas. She arrived with all this and more and even got me some dinner. When it looked like I wasn't going to get into a regular bed, Kristi left and I tried to get to sleep. It was impossible, but by 9:30 p.m., a bed became available and I was put in a room with another patient on the other side of the curtain.

I tried to sleep but they kept taking my blood pressure. Finally in the early morning hours around 6:00, I was left alone. And then I felt abandoned. No one came to give me breakfast or tell me if I was able to go home. I finally talked with one of the nurses who was attending another patient and she sent in a nurse who apologized and said they didn't know I was there. Someone had failed to put down that I was admitted late the night before. I finally got breakfast and before long was told I could go home. I called Hugh and he came and picked me up and somehow I was able to sit on my right side long enough to get home. The hematoma that had built up on my left bottom kept me from sitting comfortably for two weeks!

After two weeks my leg was twice the size and black and blue from top to bottom. My doctor told me to think of it as being in a bad car accident and instead of spilling my blood on the sidewalk, I bled internally. And did I bleed! I'm still on blood thinners from my mild stroke ten

· ·

years ago. Eventually, however, the blood was absorbed, the swelling went down.

Many from King's Class brought in meals and other goodies that were a wonderful help for Hugh. Wendy came for a week and cooked up a storm and left us frozen meals we enjoyed for a couple of weeks after she left. She was a lifesaver!

When it was evident I wouldn't get back to teaching ESL for a couple of months, I felt I should resign and let my students get a new teacher. Hugh, too, felt I needed a longer time to recuperate. My class was absorbed into another class with a great teacher and they adjusted quickly.

I've been thinking a lot about these "assignments" God gives me. Like teaching ESL and having that Korean Bible study for such a short time. Over the years it seems God has called me to get involved with various people and then moved me on. At times I've hesitated thinking I just can't get this involved. Or this may go on forever and I'm going to be too tied down. But I've learned something interesting from Jesus' own ministry.

In Mark 1:35-39 we have an interesting account of Jesus, while it was still dark, going off to a solitary place to pray. He had a tremendously busy day the day before. I'm sure He was feeling depleted, weary and in need of His Father's strength. While He's in this place by himself, Simon finds him and says, "Everyone is looking for you." Ever felt that way? Seems everyone wants a piece of you. Well, Jesus must have had those same feelings. And He said, "Let us go somewhere else—to the nearby villages—so I can preach there also. That is why I have come."

It hit me that Jesus knew when it was time to move on. There were still needs in Capernaum, but he also knew there were needs elsewhere and His Father wanted Him to go to Galilee as well.

I remember when we were first married, an old man who lived across the street came to our door, obviously very ill, and he asked if we'd call the doctor. He was so weak we told him to lie down on our bed until the doctor arrived. I can't remember what the diagnosis was. Perhaps flu. All I remember is that he felt he didn't have the strength to go back to his own home directly across the street. As he had our bed, that night we slept on the living room floor on just a quilt.

In the morning, he was not about to leave. I suppose he liked us taking care of him. After another night of this, however, we told him we would help him get into his own bed and we would bring over his meals until he got better. With much persuasion he finally agreed.

Oh dear! You should have seen his home. I don't think it had been cleaned in months, perhaps years. I cooked his meals for about a week, and in between, Hugh and I shoveled the dirt out of his house. I kept thinking, how long is this going to go on? Well, do you know, the next thing we knew some relatives got him and we never saw him again. Our "assignment" was done. It was time to move on.

A similar thing happened here at our home in Santa Ana. New neighbors moved in directly behind us. There were two young children and one day I found them sitting on our front porch. No knock, just sitting there. They said they were waiting until their mother got home. I brought them in and gave them some cookies and milk and didn't think too much about it until the next day. There they were again. When I asked where their mother was, they said they didn't know but she had told them to just go over to the Stevens place and wait.

I thought it strange the mother wouldn't ask if this was an okay arrangement, especially since we might not always be here, so when we heard some stirrings next door I walked back with the children and told the mother I didn't mind having the children, but she should check with me first to make sure we're there. She was unanimated and didn't offer a "thank you" other than an "okay."

The next day after school, the children were on our porch. I didn't know what to think but around supper time I went next door thinking the mother would be home by then. No one was there. The father was in the military and I had no idea if he was in the area or not. Thankfully he showed up around 9:00 p.m. but the news was not good. He said his wife had a mental breakdown and he wondered if we could keep the children until he could make other arrangements.

He sent over a few clothes and I was thinking the children would be with us for perhaps a couple more days. We still had Lee and Karen home so I gave the boy and girl one bedroom and Lee and Karen slept in the other one. This went on for two weeks. I wondered how long I might be obliged to look after the children who by this time were calling me, "Mom."

Another week went by and finally the father came to get the children and took them home. The next day they were all gone. They had moved out completely. No good-byes. No thank you. My "assignment" was done. It was time to move on. I've always been glad I welcomed the children and gave them some stability during what must have been a confusing time for them.

I've already told you about the movie star that was in my life for six weeks and then I never heard from her again. And Maggie, whom the Lord took home after I had spent several months reading to her once a week. And then there was Bea Klassen, the wife of a former Wycliffe Mexico Branch Director, Howard Klassen, who had been bed-ridden twenty years. We knew them in Mexico and had kept their three children once for three weeks. Now, with the children married and out of the home, they had moved to Santa Ana for Howard to retool and become a Wycliffe counselor.

This was in 1979, the time when Jocelyn and Wayne Cameron from Calgary, Alberta had bought a house a few blocks from us. Hugh didn't need Jocelyn's secretarial help every day, so after I had felt God nudging me toward helping Bea, I asked Jocelyn if she'd like to help me clean Bea and Howard's apartment and then I'd give Bea a small Bible study. We did this every two weeks for several months and again I got to thinking, I wonder how long this is going to go on? I needn't have worried. God had already prepared someone else who needed help--my arthritic friend Esther Palmer.

I began visiting her the opposite weeks Jocelyn and I ministered to Bea. God knew Bea's days were numbered and again my "assignment" ended when God took her Home. This meant I was free to help Esther weekly for about ten years and then God called us up to Canada to work in Pastoral Care at Granville Chapel. Esther passed away while we were gone.

And there were two instances when I got involved in writing women in prison. One for five years; the other for three years. I received the first name from my friend Susan LaFlamme. As Deborah was a Christian, I wrote weekly encouraging her with friendship and sharing spiritual truths. When she was released, she gave me the name of another woman and asked if I'd write her. I continued writing weekly to her. Both young women, when released, went on with their lives, releasing me to move on to another "assignment."

And sure enough God gave me a former police chief to pray for who, under the auspices of the Pacific Youth Correctional Ministries, gave a weekly Bible study to young men in Juvenile Hall. It was a joy to see this work grow. He began with only five or six who came to his study, but it grew to 20 with each of them giving a prayer request that he sent out to those he had recruited to pray for him and the young men.

This prayer assignment went on for about five years, and when the chaplain stepped down, I knew it was also time for me to move on.

And now it's time for me to move on from writing my memoirs. I thought I would continue this until age 80, but now at age 78, I think this is the time for me to put down the final period, even though there are many people I haven't mentioned who have impacted my life for good. I'm grateful to all who have challenged, consoled, encouraged, corrected and been patient with me on my journey to learn how to live my life for the display of God's splendor.

As I was finishing this volume we heard the news that my dear sister Eileen went to be with the Lord on

. . . .

September 6, 2009. I was happy I had been able to visit and pray with her in June. I was able to go to her beautiful memorial service on September 12th. Because Hugh was having knee replacement surgery on the 15th, we felt it best he shouldn't go. I flew up to Seattle on September 10th, stayed overnight with Wendy & Greg. Together we drove up to Qualicum Beach on the 11th and the next day Greg gave the inspirational message and at the reception read a tribute from Hugh. It's hard to realize she's gone, but what a grand reunion we having coming!

I don't know what's ahead for me, but I know God is faithful, worthy to be trusted and has planned good for me. Oh, the good He's planned may, from my point of view, seem unbearable at times, but there's someone from the 17th Century whose words have helped me face the future with confidence in my Lord.

In his little book, *The Practice of the Presence of God*, that came out more than twenty-five years ago, he wrote:

> God knows very well what we need and all He does is for our good. If we know how much He loves us, we will always be ready to face life—both its pleasures and its troubles...It's all in the way you look at them.

This obscure, humble monk is known only as Brother Lawrence, but when I read his words and how he felt he could worship God while washing dishes as much as if he was on his knees, I knew I had to listen to what he had to say. It was a turning point in my life and I'm grateful for his wise words.

. . . .

Eugene Peterson in his paraphrase *The Message*, writes in the Gospel of John 1:14: "The Word [God] became flesh and blood, and moved into the neighborhood." I'm so glad he came to live for a while among us to not only forgive my sins through His death on the cross, but also show me how to be a mirror image of Him for the display of His splendor. And now He's gone back to Heaven to prepare a place for me so I can move into *His* neighborhood. I'm ready! I know it won't be long.

20

The Years Following

When I first wrote the preceding chapters in 2009, I thought I had told our story. I certainly never thought I would still be here at age 90! But here we are! We thank God for the years He has given us and I do want to add a few details of our lives over the past twelve years.

We have now been in the same home for fifty years! And Hugh just finished book No. 35, *Finding God in the Shadows*, which is a delightful collection of stories from all his travels and many experiences that have helped us both discover God's truth and goodness over these many years together. He wanted to have this ready especially for the family as we celebrate our 90th birthdays and 70th wedding anniversary this coming summer (2021). I decided to update my book, written in 2009, so that we could have both books for our family reunion.

I won't go into many details of all that has happened in the past twelve years since I wrote this book. Enough to just praise God for His faithfulness and goodness in allowing us to enjoy our children, their spouses, and eleven grandchildren, three of whom have presented us with five great grandchildren between them!

Sadly, not everything has been joyful, for we lost Kristi, Dave's wife, on August 2, 2018 to cancer, and two years later on August 21, 2020, David Jr., Dave's oldest son, was taken to glory due to heart failure. Dave had so enjoyed his oldest son David, Heather and their two children, his only grandchildren, Luke and Kaylee, living close by. Sadly, now with David Jr. gone, Heather and the children have moved to Oregon to live with her parents and will be moving to Idaho later this year (2021).

As for us "old folks," our health has been good, for which we praise God, although Hugh has had difficulty with walking. (Did he just wear himself out in Mexico City buying supplies for missionaries?) Two years ago he began having difficulty getting up to his office (mentioned in Chapter 14). I was leading a home Bible study with five of my friends at the time. I happened to mention it, and asked for prayer. Just a few days later, after Sylvia Chang told her husband, he decided Hugh needed an electric chair. It was amazing! The company had it installed in an hour and Hugh has been using it daily with joy! Sadly, dear David Chang passed away shortly after giving us this wonderful gift.

As I close this book with the Covid-19 pandemic fading, we are still worshiping in our living room as we've watched our church services broadcast on line. For us, with two pastor sons-in-law, we often find ourselves listening to our own pastor as well as Wendy's and Karen's husbands! It's been a blessing, but we do miss seeing our friends at church and long for things to get back to normal.

We don't know what lies ahead, but I am asking God to help Hugh and I and the children to understand more and more how to live for our Savior, to know better how to obey, serve, study and live out His truths, find peace, hope and help for daily living, and live in the joy of His plans for us, His care and our future life with Him! My desire is that God's Word will continue to bring comfort, hope and instruction, strengthening, encouraging and equipping us all to walk in His light...

for this display of His splendor.